Presented To:

_____

From:

_____

Date:

_____

REVOLUTIONARY
FREEDOM

REVOLUTIONARY
FREEDOM

Anointed to Set the Captives Free:
The Declaration of Isaiah 61

Joey LeTourneau

DESTINY IMAGE® PUBLISHERS, INC.

P.O. Box 310, Shippensburg, PA 17257-0310

"Promoting Inspired Lives"

This book and all other Destiny Image, Revival Press, MercyPlace, Fresh Bread, Destiny Image Fiction, and Treasure House books are available at Christian bookstores and distributors worldwide.

For a U.S. bookstore nearest you, call 1-800-722-6774.

For more information on foreign distributors, call 717-532-3040.

Reach us on the Internet: www.destinyimage.com.

ISBN 13 TP: 978-0-7684-3891-8

ISBN 13 Ebook: 978-0-7684-8960-6

For Worldwide Distribution, Printed in the U.S.A.

1 2 3 4 5 6 7 8 9 10 11 / 13 12 11

ENDORSEMENTS

This is a book about a God who is liberating the captives. Some of us are being liberated from the ghettoes of poverty and others of us from the ghettoes of wealth. Some of us are being freed from the slums and others from the cul-de-sacs. Joey knows a God who is close to the poor and the suffering, and dares us to follow the Spirit to the margins, to get our hands dirty, and to find Jesus in His many disguises.

SHANE CLAIBORNE
Author, activist, and recovering sinner
www.thesimpleway.org

My first reaction on reading Joey LeTourneau's book *Revolutionary Freedom* was: "Wow! What amazing visions the Lord gave him!" My second reaction, and what I hope and pray will be that of every reader, was "Lord, I want that revolutionary freedom, no half-measures!"

This book will make you smile, it will make you weep, it will help you understand real freedom, and it will make you seek more of Him who has so much more for each of us than we have yet experienced or can even imagine.

This book will help you to become one of the "sons of God" (Romans 8:19) that creation has been waiting for since the beginning of time.

ANNE ELMER
Author of *Transported by the Lion of Judah*
(Published and available in the USA from www.elijahlist.com)
and in Europe from www.editionsdelasource.com

Joey LeTourneau has written a book that is unlike any that I have read before. Not necessarily fiction, not necessarily non-fiction—the best way I can think to describe it is a vision memoir. Deep, powerful, humorous, gripping—these stories will lead you on a journey that will leave you as a very different person from the one you were when you began.

STEVE YOHN
Pastor, Strasburg Community Church
Co-author of *Monday Night Jihad, Blown Coverage,
Blackout,* and *Inside Threat*

Here is a book from a man graced with an intimate walk with the heart of the Lord, a man whose heart has been illuminated with His light. The pages of the book you are holding resonate with the loving cry of the Lord, calling us toward His love and grace. Here, the Lord calls forth a generation that overcomes the deception of the enemy through His light...a victorious army knit together and made whole in His love.

MENELIK TAMRAT
Pastor, Covenant Church, Addis Ababa,
Ethiopia and Conference Speaker

To proclaim freedom for the captives and release from darkness for the prisoners (Isaiah 61:1).

CONTENTS

INTRODUCTION

MANY OF US ARE at a crossroads. We are hurting, but we have hope. We are trying to walk forward, but meet constant resistance. We believe God has better things ahead, but the wait seems to continue. We want more of God, yet we are plagued by the limits and torments of fear, guilt, insecurity, and a past that keep us from crossing over into God's best. We remain captive in our own thoughts and perceptions and often hold ourselves back from the fullness of that for which God has created us.

Sometimes we try to hide this captivity, run from it, and often compensate for it in any way we can find. But now is the time to shift from this captive-based lifestyle and embrace the calling God has ahead! Now is the time when we must take a step of faith toward the promises of God—and most importantly, toward God Himself.

There is a generation of God's children who live in an unseen captivity. Many of us are caught in this place. Many of us keep ourselves in this place. But God is calling us to take a step. I must take a step.

Believe Him, leave your own captivity behind, and join God as He sets forth to release the captives. Do not feel alone. You are not alone. You must not be ashamed or hide your captivity, but must bring it out into the light.

Look at Moses, one of the greatest heroes and examples of our faith. Even Moses was a captive right up until the time God used him so powerfully. Moses's transition in life from a captive to more than a conqueror shows us an amazing picture of someone who left behind his own self-sustained prison to join the Lord and release an entire generation of captives.

If we are going to understand God's emphasis on releasing the captives—the very mission for which Jesus gave His life—it is imperative that we see the transformation God brought forward in Moses's life. Moses was plagued by insecurity and fear. He could not take his eyes off his past long enough to see God's present and future. He was confronted with an impossible situation that could not be overcome by mere man. But God had a plan! He would release Moses from his own captivity and bondage and then use that testimony in Moses to release many others.

Moses helped release captive Israel from its bondage in Egypt by simple faith and obedience, but not until he himself was free. Before Moses could release the captives, he had to leave his own captivity. He had to take his eyes off himself, put his eyes back on the Lord, and then step forward. Like Moses, we cannot begin to release others unless we ourselves have gone from being *captives* to being *"more than conquerors"* (Rom. 8:37).

When Jesus began His ministry, He reached over, grabbed the Book of Isaiah, and opened to chapter 61 (verses 1-3). He read the words now recorded in Luke's Gospel:

The Spirit of the LORD *is upon Me, because He has anointed Me to preach the gospel to the poor; He has sent Me to heal the brokenhearted, to proclaim liberty to the captives and recovery of sight to the blind, to set at liberty those who are oppressed; to proclaim the acceptable year of the* LORD (Luke 4:18-19 NKJV).

At that time, Jesus began something He now calls us to continue. Even then, Jesus could see the testimony of Moses forming within us today. Jesus began a mission toward multiplication that has reached into the present. Jesus started a testimony that He has called us to pick up and carry forward. But before we can do that, our broken hearts must be healed. Our oppression must become freedom. We must have new eyes that see from His perspective, and we must be released from our captivity.

As you embark on the journey described in this book, I ask that you would open your heart to the Lord. Fix your eyes on Jesus and allow the Spirit of God to bring His Word to life in your heart. Allow the Lord to challenge and broaden your perspective of the circumstances, situations, and people that surround you. Trust God to shatter any and every prison cell that needs shattering. Walk forward and believe God for more! And as you take this journey, tune your heart to the Spirit of God and continually ask Him one question: *What do **You** want to show me today?*

Chapter 1

THE PRISON

I TOSSED FROM SIDE to side, uncomfortable and wavering as to whether or not to get up. My eyes were foggy as I rolled out of bed in an unusually unpleasant way. Voices all around me were yelling, their sound slicing through a disturbing clamor in the background. My eyes hadn't quite focused yet, my skin was clammy, and I could not stop shivering. I stumbled from bed and heard the loud clanging of metal against the ground. I fell down immediately and abruptly hit a hard, cold cement floor.

Finally, I pried my eyes open wide enough to see my surroundings. I could not believe what I saw, nor could I believe all that I was feeling. The atmosphere was piercing, like a cold, empty shriek that coursed through my being. My insides felt it more than I did externally.

Something had gone terribly wrong. Cold chains bound my hands and feet and would not give an inch. I was afraid and confused. Nothing was as it appeared to be. I cried out for help, but my cries only blended in with the yelling that surrounded me. I grabbed the bars in front of me and found them to be unusually strong. It was no use hiding the fear I felt; I just needed to figure out where I was and find a way out.

I scrambled frantically for an exit, digging at the floor, pressing the walls, doing anything I could find to do. I fell down again and tripped over my chains as I inspected the walls. I pushed and prodded for anything that might promise a way back to the reality I had always known, a way back to a comfortable place where I could finish my sleep. But I was trapped, captive in a place I didn't even know existed. I fell to my knees, disheartened, completely discouraged, and bound on every side.

My questions and fears kept increasing, seemingly multiplied by the darkness all around me. Memories and pictures began flashing through my mind. The more I thought about where I wanted to be or dwelt upon the darkness, the more overwhelmed and trapped I felt. Just the look of the walls made me feel as if there was no hope.

CHOW CALL

"Lunch!" A voice cried from behind me.

The interruption brought me back to my senses a little. An object scraped loudly across the bars of my cell and made its way down the rest of the cells. The bars opened and I carefully stepped into the dim light of the walkway. Before I could stop myself, I had filed into line with other prisoners. I struggled to walk; the chains limited my feet to little more than a shuffle.

My eyes scanned those around me, and ran back to myself. Everything seemed to point my eyes back to me. As I joined the other prisoners, I was surprised by the differences among us. In every prison I had ever seen in the movies or on television, uniformity prevailed; the prisoners looked the same, both in their dress and their chains.

We, however, did not. All of us were draped in chains, but the hardware bound different parts of our bodies. I wanted to know why. I *had* to know why! The place defied any notions I had of what prisons looked like. For that matter, it defied any notion of what I thought my life looked like. The place was without comparison. Still, I had no idea where I was. It seemed too real to be a dream. It looked like a giant maze.

We continued on our way to the dining hall, traveling through one corridor after another. Some of us walked, others shuffled their feet, and some even hopped. Several prisoners had to be carried. The degree of mobility appeared to depend upon the manner in which the chains bound each prisoner.

We were all dressed according to our unique looks and personalities, but what I could not get over were our varied chains. Some wore more chains than others. Often, the chains were placed in unusual and even painful-looking arrangements. It seemed that each chain had been carefully and strategically placed. Yet, most everyone seemed fairly oblivious to them, as if no one even knew the chains were there or that we were in prison.

Finally, we reached the dining hall. I was so happy! At least food would be something normal, and I was starving. A sign directly above our line declared: "Mess Hall." As we entered the doorway, I realized that it was more than ideally labeled. The line proceeded through what looked like a buffet. The only difference between this and a typical buffet was the fact that the Mess Hall workers chose and served our food, not us. As the line progressed, I waited my turn and noticed that the foods were of many varieties. All of it was plain-looking, and to my stomach's chagrin, none of it had any appeal whatsoever. Its stench didn't help, either. It smelled and looked like they were feeding us garbage.

As my turn approached, I paid special attention to the man ahead of me and watched what the workers put on his plate. I hoped that I might receive the same thing, as he seemed to get the best of the slop. Instead, my plate was heaped with a horrendous pile of gray-looking garbage. It released a smell potent enough to ruin my appetite for life. Perhaps that was its purpose.

"Why did I get this food when the man in front of me got something else?" I asked the worker in front of me. "What he got looked much better. I'd like what he got, please."

The worker snapped back at me in a calm but demoralizing tone, "You will get what you deserve!"

I shuffled away to find a seat, feeling as if every step was being scrutinized or criticized. I became even more defeated and discouraged. As I scooted away, the worker's comment repeated itself like a ticker tape running through my mind, making me feel increasingly insecure. As the encounter replayed in my mind, I felt an immediate tightening at my knees and fell hard onto the messy floor. My meal was scattered all over the cold cement and I fought off tears from the embarrassment. I looked down and realized that the binding feeling around my knees was the result of yet another chain.

With the added fetters, I really couldn't walk anymore, so I hopped to an open seat and licked what was left of the gray-looking garbage from my fingers. I observed the prisoners around me, hoping to better understand the place. The table was full of inmates; I was surprised when I realized that they were of all ages, genders, and ethnic backgrounds. Women, children, men, and even grandparents—all of them faced a similar fate in this prison. However, I was a little surprised that no one treated me like a newcomer. I felt as though I had just arrived, which would seem to make me a target; yet they ignored me and acted as though they had seen me there for years.

BRUTALITY IN WORDS

Very little interaction occurred among the inmates. There was a lot of yelling, and you could tell that groups gathered in cliques, often according to the ways in which their chains bound them. However, even in the cliques there was very little conversation to draw groups together. Instead, there seemed to be a shared, quiet comfort level. I kept watching and listening in on the tables and various groups dispersed around the Mess Hall. I didn't have anything to eat anyway and thought maybe I could learn something about the place or how to get out of it.

After listening for a while, I noticed that the only interaction between inmates came when one insulted another. Most of the insults stemmed from jealousy over the food someone else had been given. Very few prisoners actually enjoyed what was placed before them, and many bickered about what they would have preferred instead, just as I had. Occasionally I witnessed a trade, but everyone remained deeply discontented, and most seemed suspicious of trades altogether. The prisoners responded to each other only with harsh words, often insulting or belittling others. I wondered whether the issues bothering all of us had more to do with our perspectives of our provisions rather than what each actually had or did not have.

A woman proposed a trade to a man sitting near her; he stood right up and spit in her food. He completely demeaned her, shouting, "You have nothing to offer me!"

The woman proposing the trade was instantly bound by another chain. Her arms were yanked behind her back and bound in a new, awkward position. She stumbled away from the table distraught, with tears running down her cheeks. Her pain and response reminded me of a young child. I ached for her and began to follow her in a hopping manner down a Mess Hall aisle, wondering if I could help.

"Di...Di...Ding!"

The broken-sounding bell stopped me in my tracks. I froze, concerned about what would happen next. The ringing was accompanied by a loud voice. I could only assume it was the warden yelling out as he stood before us. I had heard others whisper about him during our meal.

"Back to your cells!" the warden yelled unmercifully—not with disdain, but as though he enjoyed what he did. I had never felt less valued, and his presence made me feel even more captive.

I blended back into what was a very staggered line of inmates, weaving through the hallways and following those in front of me. The further we were led, the more confused I felt. My emotions defeated any hope or thought of escape I might otherwise have mustered.

EACH CELL A PRISON

When we finally arrived back to our cells, I inspected every detail of mine. Again, I was used to cells being uniform in structure. However, this was no ordinary prison and these were no ordinary prisoners. The cells were all unique, but each shared at least two common qualities. Each cell was shut up and bound by the same solid and seemingly immovable bars. The bars in turn were held up by large, towering, thick walls. Each cell seemed to be a prison of its own.

The cell doors flew open at the sound of the buzzer. I walked back into my quarters, which now seemed both unfamiliar and familiar at the same time. I was still confused about how I had gotten here and was beginning to fear just how long I might be held captive in this soul-dimming place. I sat on the floor, not knowing what to do, just staring at the walls in front of me. Before I knew it, I began to recount instances and memories in my life. They were lulling, depressing thoughts, and each one seemed to pull me down emotionally. I tried to shake myself out of it, but as I tried to look upward and believe differently, a wave of guilt flooded over me.

A fellow prisoner shuffled past my cell, likely on his way back to his own. A harsh realization hit me when I realized that I knew this man, not as an adult, but as a boy from church and from junior high school. He was someone of whom we all made fun. We weren't trying to be mean-spirited; but, now, looking back, I wished I had been more thoughtful of his feelings rather than my own. Now he was in the same prison as me. His chains were layered one on top of another all across his body. He was bound by the same chains—actually, they were *judgments*—that now restricted my knees.

For the first time, I understood a little bit of what I was seeing. There were so many chains around his heart and across his body. After all these years could he really still be bound by what we had said and done? I must have robbed him of so much freedom and so much life that I couldn't even comprehend it. What if God had planned something else for him? Could my words and actions have kept him from it? The thought overwhelmed me. I leaned toward the ground and curled up deeper into my cell. I was so ashamed of myself, and felt as if everyone else knew what I had done. Just then, I felt a new, tight squeeze around the crown of my head, like a piercing headache. But it was just another chain.

If only I could go back in time. What would I say? How could I make things different? I hoped that I might have shown him love or at least some form of acceptance. I wondered whether he would still be in this prison if I had been kind to him. As regrets raced through my mind and heart, I realized for the first time just how much power each moment, word, or thought held. My judgments were his chains, and they had become my own chains as well.

I became more and more certain that this was what this prison was all about, yet I knew there had to be more. I wanted to understand it and find my freedom. There was so much oppression; the accusation and criticism were so strong that I was afraid to find out what else was going on. However, my biggest concern became the question of how long I had been imprisoned without knowing it.

Sadly, it didn't feel like a mere bad dream anymore; there was something very real about where I was. I lay there in tears for a while, pondering all I had just experienced. My emotions ran rampant. I was amazed to see how the simple words we utter affect others in such drastic ways. I felt so much shame. But then I found something (or *someone,* for that matter) that I had ignored since coming to this place: *prayer.*

I had completely ignored fellowship with God. I cried out, "Lord, please forgive me for not coming to You sooner. Help me! Please forgive me for any ways in which I judged this man. Please break his chains, Jesus, and help him to know how much You love him. Please heal his wounds and restore all the spots where his chains have chafed for so long. Lord, please let him know that You not only love him, but You love him unconditionally. And Lord, please restore the purposes for which You made him—purposes I may have discouraged him from fulfilling. I'm sorry, Lord, for all I've done. I love You."

Soon after I finished praying, I heard a clanking sound. I looked down to see metal crashing to the floor. One of the chains had fallen from my feet. To say I was relieved would be a gross understatement. I realized that the more I prayed for others, the more I took my eyes off myself and my circumstances. As I looked to God in prayer, my chains continued to fall off.

My own captivity was directly tied to the chains of others! I didn't totally understand it yet, but I was overjoyed by the hope of helping others find the same freedom that I was trying to find. I didn't want to pray for them just for the sake of being loosed from my own chains; my desire was to empower others to the same degree that I had apparently succeeded in binding them. If only they could feel free to move and to live as God had created them to move and live! Maybe they were like I had been until that moment. Maybe they had no idea they were in prison.

All I could think about was this new revelation. It was almost enough to make me forget the prison and the chains that still bound me—almost.

THE PRISON OF SELF

As difficult as my circumstances had become, I felt renewed and strangely excited. But all too soon, my feelings were dampened. I noticed something I had failed to see until then. I looked beyond the bars to where a guard stood in front of my cell with his back to me. From my vantage point, it looked as though each cell had its own guard. I had never seen a prison with personal guards for each cell. However, because nothing else here was as I thought it should be, I chose not to worry about it. Instead, I would try to understand it.

Somewhat proud of having regained at least partial freedom to move, I tried to get my guard's attention. "Guard! Guard!" I shouted. "Hey! Over here!"

He ignored me. It was frustrating, because I wanted him to notice me. I wanted him to know that the prison was losing its power over me. Yet he continued to ignore me. I picked up one of the chains that had fallen off of me and threw it toward his feet. I assumed that this would get his attention, and I was right.

I walked up closer to the bars and watched as the guard bent over to pick up the chain I had just tossed his way. As he turned around, my color drained. Whatever freedom I had managed to regain quickly turned to frailty. His image shocked me. He resembled me—*exactly*; it was as though I were gazing into a mirror.

The guard looked me in the eyes and I shuddered. I was even more afraid and confused than when I had first awoken and fallen to the floor. He grasped tightly the chain I'd thrown at his feet. He then stepped right through the bars and wrapped the chain around my knees.

The shock of seeing the guard's face was almost too much to handle. I quickly recovered and realized that although I was discouraged by the rewrapping of the chain around my knees, something else troubled me even more: I might be the only one keeping me imprisoned. The chains and the cell were one thing; I could get past them. But how could I get past *self*? The thought was almost more than I could bear. I lay there motionless and depressed, staring down the long prison corridor.

I stumbled from thought to thought, my mind eroded by the past. How and why would I keep myself in prison? How could I, or would I, ever get beyond myself?

My circumstances commandeered my thoughts. I rehearsed my present difficulties, each detail becoming magnified as I did. Just moments before, I had felt so strong. Now, the more I thought about what happened, the more my faith weakened. The bars that held me captive increased in number, each one growing wider in circumference. I didn't understand what was happening, yet I realized that as my faith spiraled downward, the bars became more formidable. Next, the walls began inching forward, further diminishing my faith. I seemed caught in a vicious cycle, a captive in my own mind.

I had to break the cycle. I had to believe! I stooped to the floor in thought. The bars kept growing. The walls kept moving. What I needed to grow was my faith, but that wasn't happening.

"Lord!" I cried out. "I give You my thoughts. Please increase my faith!"

Once again I was amazed at just how quickly I withdrew from God when negative circumstances presented themselves.

"Lord," I whispered again. "I love You."

A simple hymn echoed throughout my heart and found its way to my lips. The more I heard it, the more I began to believe again. It brought to mind the story in the Book of Acts about Paul and Silas in prison (see Acts 16:16-40). They praised God in their awful circumstances, and God rescued them. I had to believe the same would be true for me.

I began to sing to the Lord, "I love You, Lord…"

Immediately, my faith was strengthened.

"And I lift my voice…"

Light entered my cell.

"To worship You, oh, my soul, rejoice…"

Chains began falling to the floor.

"Take joy, my King…"

The walls receded.

"In what You hear…"

The bars began to disappear.

"May it be a sweet, sweet sound in Your ear."[1]

I praised God over and over again until all the chains were loosed from all parts of my body. As I lifted my head, a smile from the deepest part of my heart rose to my lips. The bars that had held me captive were gone.

I wasted no time pondering what to do next. I just started walking, pleading with the Lord for more grace and direction. He responded by giving me unusual peace. I picked up my pace and ran from hallway to hallway, searching for any exit that would take me out of this maze of confusion.

It was as though the Holy Spirit hovered right over my shoulder. He whispered to me, move by move, as I darted left…then right…then straight down the hall. I tried not to look back or too far ahead. I just listened for His voice in my heart.

He continued to bathe me in His peace as I arrived at a door marked "Freedom?" I opened the door, but just before I walked through it, I glimpsed down the corridor to my right. There the warden stood with his piercing eyes and wicked voice. He didn't yell, but he called out to me, almost jeering, "You'll be back. They all come back."

I stepped out the door and slammed it shut with a sigh of relief. The freedom and joy in the Lord felt like wings to my spirit. I determined never to allow myself a trip back to that place.

"Thank You, Lord," I murmured, feeling very tired.

I slumped down to the ground, closed my eyes, and slipped into a deep sleep.

Chapter 2

THE WARDEN

"YOU'LL BE BACK," I shouted. "They all come back." I continued muttering to myself as the man left my prison.

Many people try to walk out that door marked "Freedom?". Most never allow themselves to enjoy true or lasting freedom though. It's kind of funny, really. I don't have to do very much to bring them back here. Maybe that's why I love being the warden of this prison. It gives me joy to keep these people captive, separated from the Lord.

"Oh great, you made it," I said as my new apprentice walked in. "Boy, do I have a lot to share with you. Let's not waste any time. We have a great deal to cover today."

"Thanks for having me today Mr.—um—I don't—"

"Just call me Warden."

"OK, Warden. My name is Krima."

"What an interesting name. Do you know what your name means, Krima?"

"Oh yes, I try to live out the essence of my name each and every day. You might even call it the reason for my existence. I like to think of it as a sort of gift I have. My name means 'judgment' or 'condemnation,' which is precisely why I want to study under you.

"I think it will be beneficial for me to see what goes on inside this prison, which is why I am here in the first place, right, Warden? You're going to show me the ropes, or the chains, as the case may be."

I liked the young man's spunk and found it easy to fuel his passion for the mission.

"Krima, I think you will fit quite nicely in our prison. You should enjoy what it has to offer—or should I say, you'll enjoy what it has to take away.

"We take great pride in the fact that we have many more people coming into our prison than we have leaving it each day. This is very important to us, and we wish to keep it this way. The problems begin when prisoners release themselves. When that happens, others are more likely to follow."

A SIMPLE, ANCIENT STRATEGY

"Warden, what do you mean 'when prisoners release themselves'?"

"Krima, this is the essence of this prison, and it gives me a great laugh whenever I really need one: We cannot keep anyone here. All we can do is make it easier for the prisoners to keep themselves captive. The Lord has released each one of them. He has signed their release papers with His blood. This is why we have to use darkness and all kinds of deception to keep them from even seeing the light, let alone walking in it.

"Think of it this way: How can they aspire to leave if they don't know there's something better out there? One of the greatest methods of bondage at work in this place is to use the fact that many inmates don't even realize they are held captive. My ultimate job as the warden is to keep them from believing. I don't just try to keep them from believing in the Lord. Many believe in Him and are still here. My job is to impair their vision, feed them a few lies, and keep them from living by faith."

Krima listened intently as I continued. "We have three principles here, and each is strategic. They are designed to squelch any future or purpose in every inmate's life. Deny faith, deny hope, and most of all, deny love—and I can guarantee you that this prison's population will increase with every passing day.

"You see, Krima, without faith, hope, and love, people cannot grow closer to the Lord, even if they claim to know Him. We tolerate the inmates acknowledging Jesus. Many are satisfied just to proclaim their religion as a kind of name tag. I don't mind them wearing Jesus across their chests—as long as they don't walk closely with Him in their hearts.

"The important thing is to deceive and blind these prisoners any way we can to keep them from seeing God as He is. To deny faith keeps them from believing all that the Lord wants to do in and through them. To deny hope is to keep them from believing that He has even better plans for tomorrow. And well, to deny love is to deny them the fullness of all the Lord wants to reveal and lead them into. Is this making sense, Krima?"

"Yes it is, very much so, although I must say that I am amazed at how many prisoners choose to stay here even though we can't do a thing to keep them from leaving. Especially Christians—I thought this prison was only for the lost."

"Well, Krima, that is precisely the beauty of the thing. They can be Christians. They can go to church. They can talk about the Lord all they want to. But that doesn't mean they are not lost."

TIME-TESTED TACTICS

Krima marveled as I asked, "How would you like to take a tour?"

"That sounds great, Warden."

As we walked, I gave my new friend a lesson about the prison's history. "This place has been around since the beginning. People have been in and out of here. Some stay, some go, but the place never changes. It is virtually the same today as it was at its conception.

"Our job is simple, but it takes some work to cause people to keep themselves captive here. Most of the work doesn't involve any physical labor or fighting. It's more along the lines of strategic planning geared toward the mental side of things."

My student was all ears.

"The key is to mess with people's minds. We use many different strategies to keep them from seeing God. We want them to focus only on themselves. When people think too hard about themselves or their actions, it doesn't matter whether they're positive or negative. They'll always lead toward darkness. If we can feed them lies about themselves, their pasts, or even about God, we can make them sink further into the negative, virtually immobilizing them. Sometimes we feed them lies about positive things, telling them how strong or wise they are on their own. I love it when people start to depend on themselves more than they do on God. Anytime we can stir up pride, we can sit back and expect a fall.

"Everything we do here begins in our foundation. This prison sits on the grounds of deception. Way back in the Garden of Eden, just after Adam and Eve were created, there stood two trees. One of them was the Tree of Life, which bears the fruit of life in God. We never want our prisoners to taste this fruit because it is their way out of the darkness in this place. This fruit leads to multiplication, which is what true life does—it multiplies. We can't have that!

"As much as I despise the truth, it is just as Jesus stated in His Word: He is 'the Way, the Truth, and the Life.'[1] The fruit that grows from the Tree of Life leads people to intimacy with the Lord—as long as they partake of it. It takes them beyond an understanding of the Bible and allows them to become one with the Lord whenever they choose to.

"You see, Krima, the fruit from this tree is more potent than it appears to be. To partake of this fruit is to partake of the Lord Himself, and grow in a greater intimacy with Jesus. When people spend time in His presence, it becomes very difficult to bring them back here. If they meet the Lord in this intimate way every day, it changes their vision. This is why we strive to impair their vision with lies. It helps keep them here.

"Typically, our most strategic time of the day is early morning. We must keep prisoners from waking up and going into the Lord's presence, or they will ruin the entire day for us. We must set the tone for their day with confusion, self-focus, busyness, frustration, and lies that will trap them in their own thoughts.

"We need to focus them on the other tree in the garden—the Tree of the Knowledge of Good and Evil. This is the ground of deception that we are built upon. Our tree looks very much like the Tree of Life from the outside. We have disguised it well. They can only tell the difference when they begin to see with the Lord's perspective. Once again, darkness is our ally."

My trainee seemed deep in thought.

TWO TREES

"Are you with me so far, Krima? I am about to get to a very important point. You need to understand it if you want to be established in the art of deception."

"Oh yes. I'm with you. Please continue, Warden."

"The fruit on our Tree of the Knowledge of Good and Evil teaches people all about God. It is filled and sweetened with truths from the Bible. Our fruits teach character and good works. They—"

"But Warden, why would you—"

"Let me finish, Krima, and you'll understand. We fill our fruits with virtually everything that one associates with God, but we pull out the seeds. The seeds in any fruit are what bring it life, and they can later be planted and multiplied. Without the seeds, the fruit can be enjoyed or even shared, but without much of the impact.

"See, Krima, the seeds are grace. If we feed people truth without grace, we remove the life that could otherwise be known. The removal of grace causes our subjects to depend on self rather than on God. The beginning of any life born again in Christ starts with the grace that He has given. A person's life can only be multiplied for the Lord when grace is able to pour through it to others. This is the first and largest feature in our greatest principle, which is to deny love. We teach inmates to scrutinize, criticize, and judge others by the truth, but without the grace that balances it.

"People who have only knowledge of the truth without the life of Christ can never walk with Him who is Life. It is like giving someone a lot of something good so that they never recognize their hunger and thirst for what is best. They'll feel full, yet have a craving inside that never really leaves. They can rationalize all of their good works or character, and they may know all about the Lord. They may even witness to the lost. All of this, however, falls on dry ground if they do not know Life Himself, but only know about Him.

"This fruit of knowledge fits right in with your name, Krima. We give people the truth without letting them know the life of grace. That's when they begin to judge and bind one another in chains. It makes it even harder for them to leave this place—and makes our job that much easier. It pits Christian against Christian, church against church, the saved against the lost, and so on. It divides and therefore conquers.

"Yes, sir, Jesus may have won the war, but I will keep as many prisoners of war from the victory celebration as possible. They are not even fighting against us half the time; they are fighting with each other."

I glanced down at my warden's badge and smiled wryly at my guest. "I did not achieve the name *father of lies* for nothing."

Krima hung on my every word.

DIVIDE AND CONQUER

"OK, Krima. We're coming up on the Mess Hall. I'll show you some of the lies, judgments, and the rest of what we do here. You'll see it all in action. Right this way.

"Here we are. These prisoners are waiting in line to receive their meal portion before sitting down to eat. Every person comes through here three times a day, and each time they come through we condemn them with lies and negative suggestions about themselves. We can belittle them by giving them less food than they feel they deserve. We manipulate portion size and food choices to incite envy and jealousy in their spirits.

"It is true that most inmates believe the grass is always greener on the other side. Contentment may draw people nearer to God, but discontentment helps us lead them down the slippery slope of victim mentality and division.

"Everyone here gets the same slop, but we stir it up in a variety of ways. Prisoners get upset over the amount and appearance of the food. They get insecure about what they see others getting or by how others are treated. We want to make every prisoner overly self-conscious. This way they take everything personally, as if everybody has a negative opinion of them. This causes inmates to bind themselves even further. We want them to become so sensitive to what others might be thinking that they interpret any facial expression or gesture as a judgment. We are trying to make them see things through a kind of cloud. The more they interpret ordinary inter-actions as being personal attacks or judgments against them, the more likely they are to grow embittered or judgmental themselves.

"As you can see, many of the prisoners in the line right now are eager for their turn. Prisoner self-esteem is often so low that they grasp for any chance to be noticed. Being in this line stirs up their desire to be the center of attention—even if it's only for that one second while they are being served. All we have to do is make sure the moment they have been waiting for turns out to be less than what they expected. That's all they need to sink a level deeper into their own captivity."

"I am a little confused, Warden. Why is each prisoner bound so differently? They are chained up in such a variety of ways. It's astounding! How do you decide how to bind each one?"

"You are forgetting the key to this prison, Krima. We are not the ones responsible for imprisoning these people. We cannot actually touch them. Remember, each prisoner is here because they keep themselves here. The chains they wear are patterned after the areas in which they have bound themselves.

"It actually works out quite nicely. Prisoners often get upset when they run into others who are less bound than they are. Jealousy makes them search for ways to accuse or belittle others, therefore binding both of them in yet another judgment. Once the prisoners' vision is sufficiently impaired by lies and half-truths, self-focus will cause them to dig their way deeper into darkness each and every day.

"We keep a low profile here at the prison. We want prisoners to battle self instead of us. We cannot let them know that we are the enemy, because if they stand against us, they will realize we have already been defeated. Christ stands over us; we cannot let them stand there, too. If we create dark cells around prisoners, we will prevent them from standing against us and realizing that we have already lost the war to Christ.

"We play the game of deception well. We stir dissension within their hearts so they will pity themselves, judge one another, and grow bitter toward the Lord. It is quite amusing. If they could truly see, they would realize that nothing is stopping them from joining God in the fullness of the callings on their lives. If they could see the same vision for their lives that God sees, they wouldn't just leave their own captivity—they would take hundreds, or even thousands with them. But as long as we keep prisoners caught up with themselves and those around them, we have very little to worry about. Most don't even realize they are here, let alone understand that we have already been beaten.

"Yes Krima, everything we do here is a façade to keep people from being close with God. The Lord pursues each of them relentlessly. We just try to make them see themselves more, and Him less. It is kind of a motto here: 'A façade a day keeps God away.' Nice ring to it, huh?

"OK, now. What I have told you is just some of what takes place in our Mess Hall. People come in to get fed and they walk away feeling emptier than before."

I paused to get some feedback from my walking companion. "How are you feeling about all of this so far, Krima?"

"I must say, Warden, this is quite the operation you've got going here. I'm astounded at your dedication to lies and I'm even more amazed at how easily people believe them. Most of the prisoners don't seem to know that they are limiting themselves from so much of what could be theirs. Most of all, I am shocked at how many of the prisoners here are Christians, good people who have so much more inside just waiting to be found. I think it's brilliant how well you have disguised so much in their lives. Truth without grace…what a concept. And quite the weapon."

Krima looked at me, his eyes aglow with expectation. "Warden, I would love to see the cells now—if it's OK with you."

"It would be my pleasure, Krima. Right this way."

I knew Krima would be shocked at the sight of our cells. They never look quite the way people expect them to look. "Here we are, Krima. These are our cells."

"But where are they? I see the prisoners, but there are no cells surrounding them. I can see their chains, but where are the walls and bars? Oh, let me guess, Warden. This has something to do with the fact that they imprison themselves."

"Bingo. That is very astute of you, Krima. You are picking up on all of this very quickly."

Satisfied with my new protégé's discernment, I explained further the brilliance of our system. "There are no cells built with walls or bars that can be seen by any eye but the prisoners' own. They can see their own prisons because they put themselves there. They also see the cells of the rest of the inmates.

"Like I said back in the Mess Hall, insecurity is a major building block around here. It is often insecurity that makes people judge or accuse one another. Insecurity brings about faultfinding, judgment, and even condemnation. The prisoners can see one another in their cells because they try so hard to see each other there. No one wants to be the only one, so they look to see the negatives in each other. That's how they comfort themselves. This turns the whole process into a vicious cycle.

"If you make a prisoner feel as if he's the only one locked in a cell, he'll usually find ways to ensure that he *won't* be the only one. Prisoners—male or female—will in fact help to build cells around each other without even realizing it. It's very similar to how the inmates bind each other with chains.

"The thing is, Krima, that most prisoners feel trapped; they just don't know what is holding them. They can easily walk through their bars, if they would only believe. That is why we work so hard to remind them that there is nothing to believe in. We deny faith and they get busier erecting their bars. They simply trap themselves in their own unbelief.

"Each person's walls are only as big and thick as they choose to believe they are. To most prisoners' minds, the walls extend beyond eternity and seem impossible to get through. The farther they allow their walls from the past to extend, the more they subject themselves to darkness. Guilt and shame run rampant between their walls and make them feel even lower. It works out nicely for us; it's a helpful turn of events. The more guilt or shame they feel, the less they are able to believe. The weaker their faith, the larger the bars look.

"Prison is about routines, Krima, and that is exactly how we want it to be. If we keep everyone feeling like things are OK in their daily patterns and we keep them contained in their familiar little boxes, they will be completely limited."

"Warden, this is great. I can't thank you enough for all of this. There is so much to learn and so much I can practice in the art of deception. I never knew how powerfully such little things could affect people without their even knowing it. I would love to hang around the prison for a while, if that's OK with you."

"It's fine with me, but I still have one more place I want to show you."

THE SUBSTITUTE FOR "BEST"

Krima looked perplexed. "What is this?" he asked.

"This, my young apprentice, is The Yard. We periodically allow prisoners to come out here and see a little more light than they are used to. Being outside in The Yard here gives them the feeling of freedom. Because it's a little bit more than they are used to, they become content with it. In reality, of course, it is false freedom. Our hope is for them to believe that this is as good as it gets for them. In a sense, The Yard will deny them hope for all that is really possible with God. How can you hope for more if you think you already possess all that there is to be had? Oddly enough, freedom is actually a prison in itself—outside of true freedom within the Lord, everything else is false.

"In The Yard we give our prisoners the opportunity to make choices, to speak freely, and for the most part, to do whatever pleases them. This looks like tremendous freedom to them because it allows their minds and emotions to reach far beyond what they experience in their cells. We help them to believe that they have achieved freedom here. But truth be told, freedom is a choice, not an achievement. The only choice they can make that will give them true freedom is to choose Christ—*in everything*. If they choose to surrender only some areas of their lives, freedom eludes them. To be really free, they must choose Him at every step.

"The irony is that most people return from The Yard bound by more chains than they were when they left their cells. We give them the freedom to choose, but they rarely make the right choices. They end up choosing for self rather than choosing God's best. See, Krima, freedom can become a god for them, and that is exactly what we want. It keeps them from ever knowing Christ as their only freedom. The more we allow them to enjoy false freedom, the less they recognize the prison cells their lives have become. When it is combined with selfish desires, freedom can be the ultimate deception.

"Well, Krima, I am very glad to have you here. I think you have a very dark future with us. My assistant will show you to your quarters, but I must be going for now. I have to get back to the deception that is this world, or this prison for that matter."

Chapter 3

GIVING LIFE

DEEP IN SLEEP, I was caught up to the Lord and His throne. Angels surrounded us and praised Him. His presence was commanding. I could not turn my heart or mind away from Him. The Lord's nearness captivated me and left me nearly breathless. Humility gripped my soul and left me motionless. I felt so unworthy to be in His presence.

Then He reached down and gently lifted me into His lap. "My grace is sufficient for you."[1] He reminded me. "I have brought you here because I want you to know My heart.

"While in the prison, you experienced the effects of judgment. There is a lot more I need to show you—if you will follow Me and listen carefully. Right now, though, we'll stay here."

Unable to speak, I nodded.

"You have finally realized how limited human sight is."

"Yes, Lord, I have. But at the same time, I have begun to see things that I have never seen before. I can only imagine what else is out there. When I was in the prison I saw chains on people that

I'd never noticed before. I saw people held captive in places that I would never have thought possible. I saw the chains I was bound by—chains I had no idea were there. Most of all, Lord, I saw how the chains are wrapped around us. Slander, criticism, gossip, and all different types of judgment bound people—both the people against whom the judgments were directed and the people who sent them. Everyone who placed a chain on someone also became bound in its grip."

"You did see a lot. I'm glad your time wasn't wasted. Was it worth it to you?"

"Lord, what do You mean? It was agonizing! I don't think I can even describe how horrific a captivity it is. But, yes, it was worth it. Otherwise I might never have known that I was in the prison, or why I was there."

"The measure you use to judge others is the measure by which you will be judged," He said. "You cannot judge those around you without being judged yourself.[2] When you limit one of My children, you also limit yourself. You were able to see these things for the first time because I gave you a glimpse of My perspective. You must learn to see with this vision at all times. Judgment is much more prevalent in the world and the Church than you realize. It is a form of accusation that condemns and breeds death rather than life.

"Judgment is highly deceptive. It comes and goes as easily as an opinion changes. Job's friends judged him based on the extremity of his circumstances. Instead of loving him and praying for him unconditionally while he battled, they chose to judge him. They thought that hard times were surely brought upon his life by his own doing. They applied common sense and even truth. But they did not know My heart or his obedience. They did not know what

I might be doing in or around his life. None of you has the right to judge another at any time or in any way. There is never a reason or exception that allows you to do so. Often, when My children think they are trying their best to help someone fix a problem, they are actually adding more chains."

TRUTH, GRACE, AND JUDGMENT

The Lord continued, saying, "The world had truth since the beginning of time, but when I came to the earth I brought grace.[3] It is important in your relationships that you not only bring others before truth, but also into My presence before Me. You may come boldly before the throne of grace.[4] This is where hearts are healed.

"Judgment is rooted in the accuser himself. It is one of the strongest and most deceptive forces in the world. It creates division between you and others. More than anything, it creates division between you and Me. Judgment is one of the largest and most detrimental powers in the Church because it keeps Me away from My Church. This must not continue."

I was taken aback by what the Lord shared. I was still trying to process it when He continued speaking. "It all goes back to the Garden of Eden and the first man and woman of My Creation. Adam and Eve lived in the world of perfection that I created for them to enjoy. Once sin took hold of them, they had a new perspective. Their vision changed from that point forward.[5]

"When sin remains in your life, your vision is clouded. This relates to My command to be in the world, but not of it.[6] With sin, the world starts to take possession of your vision. After Adam and Eve ate of the Tree of the Knowledge of Good and Evil, they began to see from the world's perspective rather than Mine. This was apparent when they became self-conscious of their nakedness and took on new insecurities. They ate from that tree and thus took thoughts and understanding into their own hands. I created man for the fellowship that He and I would share, but the Tree of the Knowledge of Good and Evil is a counterfeit form of knowing Me. Knowledge from the Tree of Life fills the void that only life *with Me* and life *in Me* can fill.

"Knowledge is wonderful and necessary; however, unless it is viewed from the proper perspective, it will quickly divert you from your union with Me. Are you following what I am saying?"

He read my heart before I could respond.

"After sin came to man, I came to save the world, not condemn it. Yet condemnation continues to increase. I urged Adam and Eve not to eat from the Tree of the Knowledge of Good and Evil, not because I wanted to withhold anything from them, but because I was trying to protect them. The problem with knowledge is that when you receive it, you are tempted to use it on your own. This is very dangerous. This is where judgment and condemnation are bred."

The Lord's passion for the subject was evident. The pain it brought Him was seen in His eyes.

"You see, the tree imparted the knowledge of truth to Adam and Eve, but that doesn't mean they understood it. Their sin gave them a new knowledge and view of their nakedness. It took their eyes off Me and put their focus on themselves. This was the beginning of the insecurities that over time have deepened their roots in the thoughts and perspectives of humankind. Insecurity has birthed pride, fear, and judgment. It has even brought death to those for whom I brought life. Even that which seems like good knowledge can cause man to put himself in My place, as though he were God."

FROM BLINDNESS TO SIGHT

"I have given you truth in My Word, yet most receive more teaching from people than from Me. This gives them knowledge of the truth, but fails to impart the grace that must surround it. Truth is a gift from Me, but you and others have turned it into a weapon. It is often used to judge self and others, and to tear down what I am trying to build up. It is not necessarily one's motive to use truth this way. As man, you try to help, but you do not always know best.

"Nothing can replace time spent in My presence to hear My voice and My opinion. I, the Lord, am the One and only Judge. I AM the righteous Judge[7] who sees the heart and therefore offers grace and life. You must trust others into My hands and allow Me to be God. As man, even with knowledge of truth, your judgments can and will do nothing but bring harm. They must be replaced with prayer and blessing. How often do you use My truths as a measuring tool for others rather than as a way to bless them into My calling for their lives?"

The Lord continued, "To truly embrace My Way, My Truth, and My Life, you must begin to see from My eyes. This is not easy while living on Earth. It requires a great amount of love, trust, and listening. Come with Me. I think this will help you understand."

After a long walk we stopped and approached a man who was standing alone. The Lord greeted the man with a hug and looked over to me. "I'd like you to meet Paul, the apostle Paul as you probably know Him. He is one of My greatest teachers. Why don't you spend some time together to talk? I'll be back shortly."

I was stunned at the opportunity and spoke almost giddily. "It's amazing to meet you. I can hardly believe it's you. Thanks for taking this time with me."

"By all means," Paul answered. "It's my pleasure. I love to share with others what the Lord has poured into my life. I know what the Lord has begun to show and tell you. You must know that before I met Him, I bound others in chains for a living. I had been well educated in doctrine, but I never knew grace until I met grace Himself. I personally encountered the presence of the Lord, and from that moment on, I always wanted to go back to Him. That became the strength of my ministry.

"Nevertheless, you must understand that before I met the Lord, I chained people—and I mean literally—because I thought I understood truth and how to apply it."

The great apostle continued, humbly, "When the Lord met me that day on the road to Damascus, I was blinded. I could not see and I was afraid. I was so accustomed to my eyesight that I almost did not know how to function. I now know that it was very much the Lord's plan. Shortly thereafter, the Lord healed me and restored my vision. He also took the time to teach me what true vision is. I learned that He gave me eyesight as an aid, not as something on which to depend.

"It becomes natural, as we first enter the world, to allow our eyes to control both our minds and our hearts. God used this change in me to help inspire and encourage others to know that His strength is made perfect in our weaknesses.[8] What most people understand as weakness actually becomes great strength when approached correctly. Being blinded caused me to ask the Lord for vision. I was forced to trust in His perspective and in what He told me, rather than what my eyes told me.

"I'm sure you've heard the term 'my eyes are playing tricks on me.' Well, it's not a joke. They really do play tricks on us. Satan and all his demons do their very best to lie to us through our eyes so that we will never see things as they really are. The only way to overcome this is to ask the Lord constantly to show us each person and each circumstance through His eyes. The problem is, even when we learn this most valuable lesson of asking the Lord for His perspective, we do not always take the time to still ourselves and listen to what He has to share.

"You have to trust Him and all that He tells you. Allow Christ to give you vision more than you allow yourself to see. I don't mean for you to literally close your eyes to what surrounds you. I am talking about your perception, wisdom, and discernment. You always have a choice: Either you will let yourself take over and try to give yourself these things, or you will inquire of the Lord about them. But, always, ask yourself this question when your eyes begin to relay a situation to your heart: *What does Jesus see?*

"This is what changed my ministry so powerfully. I had all the knowledge a person could ask for or be trained in. Yet, until I allowed the Lord to be my eyes and ears, I bound more people than I blessed. If you will take the time throughout each day to listen for His viewpoint regarding every person and situation, He will pour through you so that you can pray others forward and not hold them back. This is the vision He wants you to learn."

THROUGH HIS EYES

The next thing I knew, Paul was gone and I was surrounded by music. Everything was black and people were on all sides. My sight was gone and I sat in the middle of a standard church service. The worship was familiar, but the volume seemed louder than it ever did before. I believe my hearing was intensified. With my heart I looked up to find the Lord and just kept looking. I cried out to

Him, remembering how Paul had urged me to ask the Lord for His sight.

"Father, I can do nothing on my own to see. The only vision I have left is Yours. Please let me see from Your eyes those with whom You have surrounded me. May I see them as You see them instead of as the world projects them?

"Lord Jesus, please forgive me. I know I have judged so many people. I have given others more or less power simply based on what my eyes have told me. All this time, I have been using the wrong eyes. Lord, please—if only once, right now, would You allow me to see someone in Your light? Here to my right—would You let me in on Your view of these people right now? Thank You, Lord! Thank You for opening my eyes today, Jesus. I praise You, Lord!"

Just then, while looking upward with my heart, a light shone beside me.

Beautiful worship flowed freely from a man standing with His arms lifted high. I knew more than just his hands were lifted high in worship. I saw how he gave his whole heart up to the Lord in praise. His face was bent upward; its glow was defined by a sweet smile he seemed to be sharing with the Lord. Slowly, he knelt in worship. As he did, the light increased around him. He knelt there silently for a time. I don't know how long it was.

I was enamored with the spirit of this man. From his stillness, he rose to his feet and moved passionately in worship. The way he danced was surely a worship born of freedom. Nothing could hinder his heart as he sought nearness to his Lord. He began to praise with strong words, reciting the Lord's promises as praise to His God.

A whisper nudged my attention. "It's time to go. Follow Me."

My eyesight had not yet returned when the Lord took my hand and led me to the back of the room. Once there, He turned me around and leaned me back against the wall. "Open your eyes and see," He stated.

When I opened them, I scanned the congregation through the light. I looked for the man next to whom I had stood for so long. Where was this worshiper whom the Lord had helped me to see? I walked back toward the front of the room, trying to calculate the distance we had walked so I could get a sense of where the man might be.

Hearing my thoughts, the Lord whispered, "Second row. He is on your left. Aisle seat."

But I saw no man in that seat. Instead, I saw a woman with her children. She was trying to quiet them down for fear of disturbing someone. I was confused for a second, until I saw him.

There he was. He was definitely in the aisle seat. In fact, he sat in a special seat of his own. The man sat in his wheelchair, moving awkwardly, with his head tilted upward. He bellowed his own words with the song, his arms moving ever so slightly. The man had cerebral palsy, a disease that kept his body captive. My heart stopped, awestruck. His body was so trapped, but his heart so free.

I looked to the Lord. Tears streaked down my face as I fell to my knees. "Thank You, Jesus. Thank You so very much, Lord, for helping me to see."

"Do you see My treasures in this man?"

"Yes Lord, I do. How could I not? How can a heart be so immeasurably different from the outside? There is so much going on inside him."

"And you didn't even see much," He chimed in.

"Is this how people look in Your eyes? I've had thoughts all these years about who people are, and now I realize that I haven't a clue. I have missed out on so many people for so long. Lord, forgive me. Jesus, forgive me for judging according to the flesh. Please forgive me for not seeing what You have created in people. Lord, only You know the heart. My assumptions, feelings, guesses, and misunderstandings of people have all been judgments that have bound them. Even when I viewed people based on some portion of the truth, I often used the truth negatively, didn't I? Oh, our physical eyes really do lie to us. Lord, I am sorry for everything. I—"

"It's OK, I forgive you. This is why I brought you here. You have seen for the first time. It is this sight that I am calling you to. This is how I want you to see everyone. My children have bound My children. My followers have stepped in the way of My followers. I will not stand for this any longer. As you choose this vision— *My vision*—you will learn a new way of love. You will see the very heart that I desire to bless in each person. You must extract the precious from the worthless."[9]

I could do nothing but listen as the Lord spoke.

"It will not always be easy because you will be called to do this with the world surrounding you and harassing you on all sides. Many will not understand. But this is the first step to blessing. I am sending forth My children to bless My children. You are called to pray them out from where their physical minds and bodies walk and into the place where their hearts have been created in My image to live. You are called to pray My people forward into the place I have created them to inhabit.

"Everyone has their own captivity in which they allow themselves and others to hold them. To see others as I see them will allow you to communicate My love to them. You have the opportunity to bless them by helping them see who they really are in Christ. That is what a blessing is. It is to communicate to them their worth in Me. To bless is to bring forth My treasures in their hearts. It is bringing out the good no matter how bad the outside may look."

With every word He spoke, my heart expanded.

"You must remember that each and every person has been created in My image.[10] To bless them means to give them faith in My love, in My value of them, and in My belief and purpose for them. When you bless people, you are giving them hope that they have a purpose in life. You are showing them the hope I have for them, and you are revealing to them the treasures they have buried inside. All people must know that My love for them is unique and special. I want you to bless others with the unconditional love I have given you. I want you to bless them with the value and worth their lives hold to Me. And I want you to bless them with belief in the purposes I have called them to.

"When you saw through My eyes the man whose body was held captive by disease, you felt and saw an intense love, didn't you? That man must know that this is how I see him. Everyone has wounds, sins, and pasts that they allow to speak to them more than they allow Me to speak to them. They would rather believe the lies of this world than the truth from their Savior. You must make known to them the real truth of My love, and you must let them know it is unconditional and passionate for them.

"So many of My children stare into the mirror the world reflects back to them. By blessing others you help them to see their reflection in Me, in My Word, and by My Spirit. True and pure vision was lost with sin in the Garden of Eden. It was replaced by focus on self. In order for My Body of followers to be what and whom I have called them to be, their vision must be restored. Blessing helps release them from focusing on self and that which surrounds self. It helps to lift their eyes again through the angle of faith, hope, and love.

"A blessing is this simple: it restores My perspective of faith in people's lives. It offers the hope that My Word and My vision promise to them. And it offers the unconditional love necessary for them to walk forward with Me in My Kingdom and My purposes. If you will bless others with Me, you will truly help the blind to see."

"Thank You, Lord. I cannot say that I am there yet, but I will continue to try. I want to learn. I want to join You in all of this. But mostly, I can feel the power and authority of Your love. I'm learning how much You ache for us to receive all You've given us. You have given us so much more than salvation. You have created us to flourish with You now, to experience Your Kingdom here on Earth as it is in Heaven.

"Lord, I can't help but think of the Israelites as they wandered through the wilderness grumbling and trying to seek their promised land. Now I know that You were their promised land. All they needed to do was choose You, right?"

The Lord looked at me with love in His eyes before He continued.

THE CRY OF THE BIRTHRIGHT

"One of the best examples I can give you from My Word is found in the life of Esau. In Genesis[11] you can read about Jacob's successful plot to receive his father's blessing. The blessing was meant for Esau; it was his birthright as the firstborn. However, Jacob knew the power of the blessing, as well as his divine need for it. He understood this so well, he would do anything to receive it.

"After Esau learned that Jacob had indeed taken his birthright, he was heartbroken. He let out a loud and bitter cry, 'Bless me too, Father.'[12] Esau knew his birthright and was imprisoned by the thought of not receiving it.

"I have created each person in My image with that same craving for Me. I am their birthright. Yet many do not realize it; they do not know that they want it. But their hearts know. Walk through the world and listen through My ears and you will hear the same loud and bitter cry of Esau: 'Bless me too, Father.'

"You said it yourself when talking about the Israelites. I AM their promised land. I AM their birthright. They must choose Me. Many Christians stay captive in their cells, much like you did. They never realize the fullness of their birthright and purpose in Me. They may miss out on much of what I have made available to them. Be careful. You must not judge those who keep themselves in this place. Instead, help them to see.

"I am not just a promised land to know about, but I AM their promised land to walk in right now. It is My desire to bless those like Esau and restore their vision of who I AM and what I have created them to be a part of. I AM answering their heart's cry, but they will not allow themselves to hear it. Some do not know where to listen. By calling you to bless, I am calling you to be My voice. I am asking you to join Me in praying forward these generations who reject themselves while I am trying to bless them."

The Lord's heart poured forth in His words.

"If only they knew how much I love them. Their hearts would no longer cry but would rejoice. There is a generation of My children in the world whose hearts cry, 'Bless me too, Father.' Yet they look to the world as their father rather than to Me. Even My followers wait for the world to meet them so they can hear what the world will tell them. But this generation must know the truth because the truth will set them free.[13] This generation of children must see with a new vision and live with the purpose I have created them for. I am asking you to join Me in releasing the captives by blessing the captives. Let not one go unloved. I am asking you to bless children's hearts with My views before they can be lied to by the world's views. They mean everything to Me. You mean everything to Me. Please show them what I allow you to see."

My thoughts raced through the journey that had been my life up to now. I couldn't help but think of all those I judged instead of blessed. I had so often brought death rather than life. It wasn't even intentional. I could bring death to others by judging them, or I could bring life by believing in them. All I had to do was believe what the Lord's eyes told me rather than what my physical eyes saw portrayed.

It was clear: The Lord was raising up a generation of knights for His army, and He was allowing us to dub them with His blessing.

It was time to pray them forward.

Chapter 4

SATAN'S GARAGE SALE

I STIRRED FROM MY rest and looked up. The unusual amount of light caught my eyes by surprise. I had never seen light in this manner; it took some time to adjust to it. The strength of the light reminded me of a summer exit from a matinee movie. It was shocking to my system and a complete contrast to what I had known in the prison. The prison's atmosphere was similar to what I was used to living in. This light, though only a fraction as powerful, reminded me of my time in the heavens with the Lord.

I would not have understood the difference in the light had the Lord not revealed it to me. I never knew how much my perspective had been lacking. I now realized that I had been in the dark for many years, though I never once felt that my vision was impaired while inside.

It reminded me of playing hide-and-seek as a kid. Whoever was "it" stayed in the bathroom to count, with the lights off and the door closed. What is striking to me now is the fact that enshrouded in the darkness of that room, I was the only thing I could see. I knew my friends were nearby, but it was too dark to see them clearly. I could not see much past myself. This is so similar to the way things are in the prison. The more we allow sin to bind us, the darker things get. I could have walked out of prison at any time but I didn't. As I sat there focused on myself, the place got darker. I had, in essence, paralyzed myself.

EMBRACING THE LIGHT

My eyes were taken aback by the light, yet my vision continued to clear up. I understood that even this empowering light could pose a challenge when it came time to leave the prison. Even a change for the positive can be overwhelming at times; the greatest things often scare us when they are outside of our control.

It was essential that I maintain the Lord's perspective. I continued to claim the verse, *"Perfect love casts out* [all] *fear"* (see 1 John 4:18 NKJV). I knew that this love was the only thing that could drive me forward.

The light changed as I began to receive it properly. In one sense, it hurt my physical eyes and was difficult to take in. Yet it was obvious that it improved my vision. I knew that it was a gift from the Lord and I had to embrace it as such. I tried to focus on all the ways He encouraged me. It wasn't easy to do, but I trusted Him.

So caught up was I in my thoughts that I forgot where I was. I hadn't moved since walking out of the prison door. Feeling a bit fearful, I looked behind me. There was nothing there! No door, no prison; all of it was gone. How weird! "Did it even exist?" I wondered. Yet, I knew it did. The Lord had specifically spoken about it.

That's when it hit me. *It was real only as long as I allowed myself to be kept there.* I had imprisoned myself in my mind and my heart; the prison was as real as my belief in my captivity.

The Lord offered me grace by allowing me to see where I was being held. If He hadn't, I might never have found my way out. What about those who don't have an experience like that? How many are still imprisoned? How will they ever find their way out—especially when most don't even know they are behind bars?

I understood a lot more of what the Lord had been telling me. Freedom has a purpose: Once we have been guided to freedom from the prison of lies, we can help others find freedom, too. He has given us that authority. That's what the blessing is all about. We can bless others with God's light to help them to see.

We are called to help others believe. The expression "seeing is believing" is contrary to the truth. It is actually the complete opposite of the truth. *Believing is seeing.* The Lord had told me as much; now I was starting to truly understand.

DARK DISPLAY

I stood up and walked into the source of the light. Excitement linked arms with curiosity; combined they led me toward the neighborhood ahead. It was a suburban area that was somewhat run down. The place was empty of life. As I walked down the street, the atmosphere became heavy. I followed the sidewalk and noticed someone ahead. I couldn't tell who it was, but she was headed toward me.

Our paths were about to cross. She was an older woman, probably in her 60s. When we drew within a few feet of one another, it appeared by the look in her eyes that she wanted to say something.

Her face was covered in concern. Her eyes were glued to my steps, and she hesitated with every move. I wondered what she was thinking, but not enough to stop and ask her. I decided it would be easier if I allowed her to continue on by. To be honest, I was glad when she did. I wanted to get on with my journey, wherever it was I was going. I could not wait to explore this new place. So I did my best not to make eye contact with the woman. I didn't know what to say to her anyway.

Eventually, I found myself in front of a sign that read, "Garage Sale—This Way." Underneath the writing was an arrow pointing to a house just down the street. My curiosity was sparked, so I decided to take a look.

I approached the garage, entered, and looked around. It was a very old house. It looked like it had been around for generations. Whoever lived there was a pack rat. The garage was dim and overflowed with boxes and old files. The heaviness in the air got even stronger as I browsed.

I had never seen a garage sale quite like this one. The items were unusual. Soon I saw the proprietor of the eerie establishment. He paid no attention whatsoever to my entrance, but I was certain that he knew I was there. He was busy with a project, so I looked around on my own. I thought it was probably better that way.

On the first table was a large crimson object shaped like a head. It had fierce eyes and hundreds of mouths. Just below the item was a sign that said, "Gossip: $1 million."

Next to this was a horrific, swollen green blob. It was one of the most hideous things I had ever seen. A sign below the blob said, "Envy: $2 million."

On the next table was a broken, black, heart-shaped device. Its sign said, "Lust: $3 million."

There were several other tables covered with a diverse assemblage of objects labeled "Greed," "Selfishness," and "Self-Ambition." I recognized each of these as weapons that had come in and out of my life at different times. They were common sins that all of us struggle with at different levels and at various times.

My heart became sick as I fumbled through the many attacks and deceptions of the enemy that were on display. I wanted to run, but I felt too tired to try. Where would I go, anyway? I hardly had a clue where I was. My mind glanced back to the image of the woman who had just walked by me. I wished I had made myself more open to what she had to offer. She might even have warned me.

Just as I thought about the good she might have done, I noticed a leather-bound book sitting on the arm of an old chair. The chair looked comfortable enough. I was tired and found the idea of getting off my feet inviting. As soon as I sat down, I grabbed the dusty old book and blew on it. As the dust flew away, I saw that the book had no title or cover; in fact, it looked more like a journal.

I opened to the first page and began reading…

FEAR'S FORTE: JOURNAL OF A FALSE REALITY

Entry 1: *My Autobiography*

Hello, how are you today? You may not know me. Well, you probably think that you don't know me. My name is Fear, and as you can imagine, fear is my forte.

The mind is a very powerful thing, you know. It can bring to life whole new realities that have no validity at all. That's my area of expertise; I control more parts of you and your friends than you will ever realize. I help you to activate your mind before you can trust your heart.

I am actually a captain in the devil's army. Did you know that I am the number-one leading cause of paralysis throughout the world? It's true. It's not physical paralysis of course. It's the kind that either immobilizes you and keeps you from coming to God, or keeps you from trusting and following God wherever He is going. It's a paralysis of the mind that trickles down to your heart, if it goes untreated. The only cure: perfect, whole, circular, unconditional, freely attained love.

The ironic thing about the growth of fear and its potential to reach an incredible size is that it only requires one little seed to get going. Once a seed finds an opening in one of my subjects, it germinates, and fear festers. The subject actually waters the seed for me. My seeds require unique conditions: They are fed by lies, and instead of needing light to grow, they sprout best in darkness and shade. The world and its perspectives prepare a better soil than I could ever dream of concocting on my own. It is perfect! The world feeds its perspectives into my subjects directly through their eyes. Luckily, they almost always believe what they see. The devil has really set me up for success.

I'm sure you've heard of my father, because I come from a very successful line in the enemy's horde. He is the foundation from which I do all my works and deception. He was involved with the original Fall of Man and even gave the devil his inspiration. His name is Pride, but he goes by plenty of other aliases. He started the Fall of Man, which has been passed on to me to finish. Sometimes I feel like a gardener with all the seeds I have to plant.

Entry 2: *My Autobiography*

Many of my subjects are on the brink of breaking out on fire for the Lord. My job is to keep them lukewarm and at a standstill. Do you know what happens to water when it is left standing? It grows bacteria and all kinds of stuff that makes it nasty, kind of like when you plug up your sink or tub.

The same thing happens to you when you're not moving closer to the Lord and constantly receiving the fresh flow of His water. You become paralyzed and your thoughts can't drain from your mind to your heart. Just think of me as the stuff that plugs up the drain. The bigger I get, the less that God's living water can flow and move. Hence, I use the word *paralysis*. It is my job to ensure that your faith stagnates. I have conceded to the fact that you will have faith, but in my opinion, your faith does not have to be alive. Trust is what gives feet to faith; trust is the only way faith will ever go anywhere or be part of anything.

I don't know whether you realize it or not, but most people (at least on some level) are doing everything they can to maintain control of their lives. Have you ever felt afraid of losing control? I hope so. The more you are afraid of losing it, the harder you will try to keep it.

Humans try to control things in a number of ways. They use caution, money, power, manipulation, persuasion, blackmail, bribery, or anything of a similar nature. You even use me, Fear. The same way I use fear to control you and your thoughts and movement, you use it to control one another. See what I mean about what one seed can do? One seed festers and—oh, man—watch out! Here I come.

Of course, fear is based in deception. Did you ever think about how remote your fear is? Stay with me here and you'll learn something. Just put together the two words *remote control* and you will realize that these words produce opposite effects. Remote control! Ever used one? I'm sure you have. Many people use them most every night, maybe even a little too much. Do you and a loved one fight over who gets control of the remote? Who gets to control the channel you will watch? Who gets to flip through the channels at their desired pace?

It has become human nature to sit in your special spot in the living room and control your entertainment with your remote control. I haven't done any formal studies on it, but it is probably one of the most commonly used tools in the world. How about that? But I must ask you, do you have control of the remote, or does the remote have control of you?

That is where I come in. Once my seed of fear grows in you, you will generally try to protect it from getting out into the light. This is exactly what I want. If I can keep the seed inside, in the dark, that's where it grows the best, remember?

When you hold the remote control, you are trying to control the television's every move so that you will not have to move. But I have to tell you that the thing that you hold in your hand actually has more control over you than the other way around. The remote control keeps you paralyzed on the couch. You are kept even from moving to change the channel—and the entertainment triggered by your control in turn paralyzes you from doing anything else.

I work in the same ways. Everyone has their fears, everyone. But many believe that if they keep me hidden and "under control," I will remain a small, remote part of their lives. Instead, I take control and use fear to limit them from being free enough to pursue their faith wholeheartedly.

People try to keep their fear out of sight. Yes, it's called *denial*. They have the nerve to walk by me all day long and look away as if they didn't even know me. Talk about rude.

Sorry, I'm getting off subject. It's just that I don't always get the credit I deserve. I guess I have a little of my father in me. But anyway, when my subjects try to suppress their fear and control where it goes, that is when I know I've got them. They think they are handling me, but I cannot be handled. I must be recognized and rebuked. The use of control stems from fear. It is evidence that I've squeezed in a seed and it's growing.

When you hold me like a remote, I will feed you false reality through whatever channel you choose. I will successfully paralyze your faith and keep it from finding its feet. You won't be able to walk, and I'll have time to grow. You must remember: You might be in control of the remote, but you're not in control of what the remote allows you to see.

Understand it yet? You will never really have anything more than *remote* control. No matter how hard you try.

Entry 3: *My Autobiography*

Control is just one of the many ways in which I manipulate my way into your life. There are vast numbers of things I can do to help you enter false reality, but I'll go into those later.

For now, I'll tell you this: I prefer to work at night. I'm nocturnal by nature. There are a number of reasons for that really, not the least of which is the whole thing with the seeds. Darkness just makes them grow with urgency. It's so nice and dark and quiet at night. You are left in the dark with your thoughts and no one to talk to. Might as well talk to me, right? I'm always ready to chat. Can't say you'll ever really get the truth from me, but it doesn't seem like a lot of people really want the truth anyway. By the way, have you seen some of those gossip magazines? Wow, if you believe those, you'll believe anything I tell you. It was actually my second cousin who inspired those writings. He's our Shakespeare, you know.

Anyway, where were we? Oh yes, I like to work at night. It's one of the only times that you humans actually get still. If I fill that time with my mumbo jumbo, then at least there won't be any room for You Know Who. I can't begin to tell you some of the things you will believe at night. I don't even need solid proof. Most people are just waiting to be influenced, but don't take the time to hear God's voice. So I just speak up.

Maybe you can help me out with something, though. I know that you hear me and you listen to me, but I don't exactly know why. Why is it that you will listen to me and my brother when God is speaking to you at the same time? Don't get me wrong, I like it this way. But I can't figure out why so many people will go out of their way to believe lies when the truth is right there, too.

Whoops, there I go again. I start talking about my brother, but I haven't even introduced him to you yet. Well, actually he's kind of like my brother-in-law, or god-brother, or something to that effect. Anyway, you've probably heard of him. Of course, my dad is partners and like best friends with the devil, who some people like to call the father of lies. Well, that's him— Lies. The devil's kid, we pretty much work together. We've become nearly inseparable. Lies is the one who prepares you for me so I can plant my seeds. I used to be jealous because I wanted to work alone. But then I realized that two are stronger than one. Do you know how hard it is for someone to get rid of Fear when they believe Lies? And there's no way people can dismiss the lies when I govern their thoughts. Sure, we have a number of other friends and family members who contribute to our fun, but the two of us really stick the closest together. We are working on a good one right now: We're slowly trying to bring faith and hope to a state of total paralysis. As long as we stick together, things are looking pretty dark.

That was it. Entry 4 was blank. But I had heard all that I needed to hear.

Chapter 5

THE INTERCESSOR

"PLEASE FORGIVE ME, LORD, for not speaking to that young man I passed by earlier today. I know You gave me a specific warning about where he was headed. All that was left for me to do, Lord, was to be obedient…and I wasn't.

"I know You shared Your warning with me for a purpose, a purpose that I neither know nor need to know. I allowed my insecurities to keep me from speaking Your encouragement to him. I was so fearful of not being received by him that I chose the comfortable route. I just don't feel like their generation wants to hear it from my generation.

"Lord, I know that thought is a judgment in itself. I know that I cannot look at the physical circumstances when obeying You. Please help me to obey You by faith, and not by sight. Jesus, I know that You are the Great Intercessor, so I ask You for Your help. You have continued to press him to my heart all day. He, along with the entire generation of young people, is heavy on my heart. Please teach me how to pray for him specifically. You promise me in Your Word in Romans 8:26 that when we cease to know how to pray, Your Holy Spirit will teach us how to pray as we ought to. Please help me to see that young man as You see him. Please help me to love him with prayers. Teach me, Lord. I'll wait here now for Your voice. I'll wait until I hear from You."

As she knelt, praying, the Lord spoke.

"Bless you, Janine. I know the obedience of your heart. I know the motives of your heart. Most of all, Janine, I know the beauty of your heart. You have nothing to fear in obeying Me. It is not up to you to cause someone to receive My cautions or encouragement. You can only share what I ask you to share or do what I ask you to do.

"Janine, your humility before Me has brought about great wisdom in your life. I have chosen you to be among the many from your generation to stand in the gap for the revival generation that I AM raising up. I have called you to wait on Me and listen to My voice for them. I want you to know how to pray for them and how to share truth and wisdom with them. I have called your generation to bless those I AM raising up.

"So many young people are being raised without their mother or father's blessing. I will give them their blessing as their heavenly Father and I will give them this blessing through many people like you. I am looking for people who will believe in My children with Me. Much of the way you will bless them is by offering them unconditional love and fervent prayers. The enemy is striving to divide the young from the old in any way possible. He will try, but he will not succeed. I know people like you, Janine. I know people like you who are willing to quiet themselves and listen to Me for the sake of another. The enemy wants to use the pride of the youth and the insecurities of the adult generation to divide a most holy union. Janine, I will turn the hearts of the fathers to the children, and the hearts of the children to the fathers.[1]

"Not only are you called to bless the upcoming generations, but you are a forerunner to your own. You must share with those like you who have obedient hearts. Remind them that their worth is in Me. You have to bless others so they can bless many more. I will bring together the generations of Abraham, Isaac, and Jacob. The youth need your balance and you also need theirs. I AM raising up a holy union.

"Think about the miracle of the increase of the widow's oil in Second Kings, chapter 4. She was asked what she had in her house to keep her two sons from bondage. She had only one jar of oil. I sent her to go and borrow as many empty vessels as possible from all her neighbors. I instructed her through My prophet Elisha to take the one jar and begin pouring it into each empty vessel that waited. She poured from one vessel to another until each empty vessel had been filled. The oil did not cease until the empty vessels were no more.

"Janine, the two sons to be kept from bondage also represent today's revival generation. You are one of the many vessels waiting on Me to be filled. I AM like the widow and will gather those who are willing to wait. I have a jar of oil. It only takes one. It is a jar of My blessing that is rich with My love. It will keep this generation from bondage and will help to bond them to Me, their Lord. Will you continue to be an empty and waiting vessel to offer this blessing of love and prayers? My oil will not cease as long as there are empty vessels waiting to receive. I am calling all who will lift off their lids so their jars may be filled.

"The more who wait on and listen to Me, the more oil will come. You must receive from Me more than you receive from the world. As long as you walk in simple obedience by faith and not sight, the oil will not cease. You are not just an empty jar, because those who are willing, like you, will be filled with some of the richest parts of Me. My two sons have no idea how much a jar can mean to them, but soon they will. Keep praying in obedience, Janine."

"But Lord, how should I pray? What should I pray? I still feel so inadequate."

"Be still and know that I AM God. Take the time to be still. Wait on Me and listen to Me. Let Me pour into you. You acknowledged Me as one who will teach you all things when you don't know how to pray.[2] When you are still before Me and focus on Me, you will be filled in a way that no church, pastor, or Bible study can fill you. All you must do is sit before Me, draw near to Me, focus on Me, and believe in what I am pouring into you. There is nothing you can do to receive these things from Me. You can only stop, wait, and rest. It is there that I will meet you.

"As you know, Janine it is a discipline to quiet yourself before Me. But there is no right or wrong way to do so. Quiet yourself, cleanse your heart with My blood so that nothing can separate us, then look to Me and wait. I will show you and tell you how to pray. It will change with each moment and every prayer. Intercession is necessary to combat the wars ahead. You and your prayers are very important to Me and our Kingdom.

"I will teach you about the wars that are ablaze and the others yet to come. The spiritual warfare ahead is of epic proportions. The enemy is bringing tidal waves of lies designed to consume My children. Many attacks will come within these waves of lies. The attacks are intended to take My children's trust and focus away from Me and place it upon themselves and their circumstances.

When you see and feel these attacks coming, you must remember that I have not come to condemn the world but to save it."[3]

The Lord's voice went silent. I sat there and thought about all He had instructed me to do. There seemed to be so much, but I knew there wasn't. It was really rather simple. I just had to do what He said, exactly as He had taught me for so many years. I had to wait. It is a discipline, as He reminded me it would be, but I know how rewarding it is. I know how powerful it is to still your heart and mind and draw near to the Lord. He does promise us that if we draw near to Him, He will draw near to us. (See James 4:8.)

I tried to stop my thoughts and separate myself from the things of this world.

"Cleanse me, Lord. Please cleanse me of anything that might separate me from You. Please draw me nearer and nearer to You, Jesus, and please cover me in Your blood. Jesus, would You please cover me in Your armor and cloak me in Your humility? Thank You for speaking to me for this time. Would You please continue? I'm here to listen. I wait on You and You alone, Lord."

He was still silent with me and I did not know why. So I waited. I waited and rested before Him until something changed.

Almost an hour went by. Then something changed. I heard nothing but silence, but I knew He was there. He had never left. How easy it is to forget that even when we do not notice the Lord's presence, He is still there. I knew He was speaking to me, but I still could not hear Him as before. He speaks to us in so many ways. Then I felt His impression on my heart. He was subtle, but powerful. I felt His love for me.

A picture appeared in my heart. It was a garage sale built around a workshop. The young man He spoke to me about earlier was in the garage and the owner of the place was satan himself. My heart broke for the young man. The Lord showed me many of the weapons and wars that surrounded him.

"Lord Jesus, I lift this child of Yours up to You. Please give him eyes to see and ears to hear. Please shed light on the walls that are his past. Please do not let his past sins hinder who You have made him to be for the future. Lord, please help him not to feel consumed by the walls and the dark shadows they cast. Please teach Him to call on You. Please send Your perfect love to cast out all fear[4] that these walls could bring back to him. Help him to trust that You are bigger than these walls. Nothing can keep him from You if he truly seeks You. Lord, please use Your light to show him Your purpose for him. Help him to hear Your voice.

"Holy Spirit, would You instill in him that simple childlike faith and trust, even as the bars of unbelief stand so thick? Help him to walk by faith and not by sight.[5] If he walks by faith, You know that he cannot be held back by any attack the enemy wages against him. The bars of unbelief can only stand when his faith is invested in his circumstances. If he trusts You above what his eyes show him, then he doesn't have to worry. Lord, please give him eyes of faith and help him to walk with them. Please strengthen his trust, Lord. I lift him up to You and into Your hands. Please perfect my prayers, Jesus."

The picture left me, so I continued to worship Him. I waited until my heart was nudged forward.

"Lord, please breathe Your living Word over this young man now. Would You claim Your promises over his life? Father, where might Your heart lie for him now? Please show me in Your Word. Where shall I go?"

I sat quietly still, focusing on Christ and listening. Isaiah 61 was brought to the forefront of my heart. I grabbed my Bible and flipped through it quickly. Isaiah 57...60...ah, 61.

> *The Spirit of the Sovereign LORD is on Me, because the LORD has anointed Me to preach good news to the poor. He has sent Me to bind up the brokenhearted, to proclaim freedom for the captives and release from darkness for the prisoners, to proclaim the year of the LORD's favor and the day of vengeance of our God, to comfort all who mourn, and provide for those who grieve in Zion—to bestow on them a crown of beauty instead of ashes, the oil of gladness instead of mourning, and a garment of praise instead of a spirit of despair. They will be called oaks of righteousness, a planting of the LORD for the display of His splendor. They will rebuild the ancient ruins and restore the places long devastated; they will renew the ruined cities that have been devastated for generations* (Isaiah 61:1-4).

"Thank You, Father, for pouring out both Your passions and Your plans in Your Word. What a powerful promise! How you can use us in these ways, I still do not know. Please precede the young man's path with this anointing. Show him what binds him so that he may walk from outward Christianity to Christ. Please do not ever let church alone satisfy him. Give him the need to pursue nothing less than all that You are, our Living God.

"You have released him, Lord, and he has begun to release himself. Like the rest of us, he judges himself far too much. Those thoughts are clearly not from You. Never let his chains become his comfortable place. The enemy would like to deceive, discourage, and depress those whom You are taking to greater freedom, because he wants to take them back into captivity and isolation. You have shown me the enemy's clouds of depression. Talk about an epidemic, Lord. What shall we pray as this comes? How can we combat its smothering form?"

I waited and listened.

"Satan is using the darkness of your past, Janine. He is using the shadows of your past to hide his deceptions in the present. I AM calling My Body together, and satan is doing anything in his power to divide. I have created each of you very uniquely. These differences have great potential beauty when they are brought together within Me. You are designed to balance one another perfectly when you allow Me the opportunity. The enemy is trying to rub these differences in such a way as to create friction instead of attraction.

"You should understand because you've done some quilting, Janine. A quilt is an odd, but cherished creation. The quilt is made up of many different fabrics or pieces that are nothing like the other pieces around them. You create them this way for a purpose. The pieces contrast with one another very noticeably, yet this is what makes the quilt beautiful. The quilt wouldn't be nearly what it is if made up of pieces that all shared the same design. It is the difference of one piece that brings out the beauty of its neighbor. The contrast is what makes them complement each other.

"Because of lies, some pieces don't see the truth. A piece might think his or her design should make up an entire blanket. Another piece might fade away because it is not bold like its neighbor. One of the biggest problems arises when one square of fabric tries to make its neighbors conform to its design.

"Instead of reflecting the beauty of its creator and representing the creator's image, the quilt begins to die. It rips, tears, snags, and further separates the beauty it was made to reflect. The pieces specifically designed to give it more life break apart from one another. Each piece loses its impact, because without the other pieces, the color pales. Each broken-off piece becomes empty and isolated.

"In this world, a piece left on its own ends up as trash that is buried in a basement or thrown away. In the darkness of the basement, its uniqueness remains, but the piece is hidden and cannot be seen. Other powers heap up trash and other items that bury the fabric even more, so that it is left untouched, without light or love. The creator of the quilt shines her light to find it, but the piece of fabric remains hidden under the weighty garbage of the past. The piece knows that it had once been chosen, but eventually forgets its special ties to the quilt's creator, who stitched it in its place for a reason. Nevertheless, hope is now lost under the burden of old trash.

"Janine, the enemy forges lies to separate the pieces of My quilt. Satan is ripping every bit of stitching he can with judgments, pride, insecurities, and much more. He wants to rob you of life so you will bring others and yourself spiritual death. He is trying to make all believers and nonbelievers entities unto themselves so they cannot be conformed to the entity that I AM.

"The enemy can divide, but he cannot conquer, and he knows this. If he cannot conquer, he will bury instead. You used the word 'smothering' when you asked Me about the epidemic of depression. This word could not be more ideal in describing the enemy's intent. Satan and all his evil cohorts are trying to take the garbage of your past and bury you. He is digging up your supposed shortcomings, your insecurities, your fears, and anything else to overwhelm you and drive you so far into darkness and captivity that you cannot see My light.

"Janine, the passage that I gave you is a way you can pray. It is the releasing of the captives. It's another example of what I have called you to when you bless others. To those whose spirits are poor and hurting, speak the encouragement and love that come from Me. To hearts that are broken, I ask you to pour in My grace and love. Give those who are held in captivity a reason to believe, and give those who are imprisoned by darkness a ray of My light.

"Bless them, Janine, with the crown of beauty that I see upon their heads. Do not let them settle for ashes. As they sink, please hold their arms and stand with them and praise Me with faith. You have been blessed by your earthly mother and father. This gives you an extra-special authority from My Spirit to bless others. The blessing is upon you. The oil is waiting to be given. All are in want and all can receive. Anyone who asks these things of Me in My name will be given them. I AM your heavenly Father, abundant in grace and wanting to give. Bless even those who curse you.[6] Let their conditions be met by My unconditional love. This is what I am calling you to bring to the generations I AM raising up. Bless these I surround you with to help Me harvest what I have planted in them. Pray them forward to join Me—to rebuild the ancient ruins and to restore and renew the ruined cities that have been devastated for generations. You are part of a holy and necessary union of generations, Janine. Again, I am calling on many like you to pray forward the revival generation I AM raising up. Don't think for a minute that you are not part of it.

"I love you."

Chapter 6

SATAN'S GARAGE SALE: PART 2

I WAS TRAPPED IN the sickness of the garage when I came across a display case with spotlights trained on it. It was a focal point in this satanic arsenal. In the display case was a simple, small, wedge-shaped tool. Below it was a sign that read: "Not for Sale. Priceless."

I wanted to leave, but I had to find out more. I worked up my strength and courage and walked over to confront the enemy and proprietor, satan himself. He looked nothing like I had imagined. He was still working on something that I couldn't see clearly.

"What's this simple, small, wedge-shaped tool over here?" I asked. "Why isn't it for sale? It doesn't look like much."

I heard a familiar, piercing laugh as satan answered. "Sir," he said, "with this simple wedge-shaped tool I have ruined marriages and destroyed families. With this small tool I have decimated churches. I've wiped out entire denominations. I have even brought whole nations to their knees. This weapon is one of the most powerful that I own, and I will never sell it. The weapon that you see as only a simple, small, wedge-shaped tool is what I like to call *Division.*"

He still would not look at me but instead concentrated hard on his project. Meanwhile, I thought about the wedge-shaped tool. I had seen the pain caused by division. I knew its impact had been immeasurable in more areas than I could ever realize or remember. Yet my thoughts were soon interrupted as my eyes fell on what lay next to the wedge-shaped tool. It was an object that resembled a hammer. Like most things here, it was not your typical household item. This hammer had many heads, each constructed in its own unique way. You could tell just by looking at it that this multifaceted object was probably used in a variety of deceptive ways.

Just as this hammer-like object lay right next to Division, I noticed that similar hammers were scattered throughout the establishment and placed next to many of the other items. The proprietor had one in his hand even as we spoke.

My curiosity prompted me to ask, "What's this hammer-looking thing? What do you use it for?"

The proprietor spoke in a deceptively soft, raspy fashion. His words were cold and far removed from love. He reeked of accusation.

He responded to me with a look of shock. Apparently he couldn't believe that I didn't know the answer to my question. "That's pride, of course!" he stated with confidence. "You can see that I'm using it right now. See these nails? Each one is a different insecurity."

Despite my disgust, my curiosity won out. I inched closer to the enemy and his project. He was working diligently and seemed to be restoring something.

"Are these for sale?" I asked.

"No," he responded. "These are antiques! I help restore them in people's lives and they grow old with them. Most people forget about the antiques still in their lives. The items just sit around their houses or in their attics or basements. It doesn't matter where they end up. Most people have a hard time parting with them."

I was about to spew out another question when I got a closer look at his project, a grouping of items. These, too, were labeled. The first in the grouping was large with incredibly thick cement walls that seemed to extend upward beyond eyesight. It wasn't for sale, but it did have a sign that read: "The Walls of Your Past." Next to these were immovable, sturdy steel bars. Their sheer presence struck me. The label read: "The Bars of Unbelief." The words were written boldly.

I felt like my head was spinning. The neighborhood's familiarity seemed to grasp at me more and more. I looked to the item in the hands of the enemy and my heart sank. I knew what I was staring at. It was the weapon I had seen used by each of us against each other and even against ourselves. The Lord had already spoken to me about this weapon; I remembered it clearly. Its use was ubiquitous, yet it escaped notice. What I was looking at were the very chains that bound me—the same chains I had put on others with mere thoughts and opinions. They were the chains of judgment.

The proprietor finally turned away from his work to look me in the eye. My heart sank even lower. My sight shifted and I saw the piercing eyes of the warden who had shrieked with laughter when I left the prison. My vision became less and less clear. I looked earnestly for the light that once seemed powerful and endless. I knew it was still there but I realized that without notice, I had veered away from the Lord. It had happened so easily as I allowed my thoughts to lead me someplace else.

The enemy laughed heartily at my reactions. I struggled to look past the circumstances and yet I let fear constrict me. Just as suddenly, the notion of grace gripped me, and I reached toward it. I called and He answered. He came to me, but I would not let Him pick me up. I was too afraid. He would not force Himself on me. "If you want My grace," He said softly, "then you must let go."

Everything seemed to crash back down on me. I didn't want to imprison myself again and I didn't walk away from the Lord. But I had relied on myself instead of Him.

Despite my mounting fear, I knew I had to change direction. I had to make a choice. I knew the beauty of the light that awaited me with Him. I knew how greatly it contrasted with the darkness surrounding me. I knew that light was where I must be. Yet fear weighed me down and blurred reality. It seemed as if the force of spiraling water was drawing me straight toward the drain. I was aware of the truth, but at that moment, I could not control it. Fear had overtaken my faith and pulled me back into captivity.

REVELATION IN CAPTIVITY

I woke up feeling as if I had been under anesthesia. But despite my grogginess, I knew where I was. There was no way to mistake the feel of it; I was back in my own personal cell—and it was my fault. I had the power to take my thoughts captive and stand on truth, yet Fear had made me his captive again. Just as Fear's journal said: He was not kidding, and I had not resisted him forcefully enough.

The grogginess wore off, and although I needed no confirmation, my eyes proved that I was in my cell. I was determined not to stay. This place could not keep me. God is bigger and I knew the choice was mine. I stood up with a rush of faith, and just as I did, a blur of footsteps passed by my cell. Before I could see who it was, I saw a piece of paper floating toward the floor of my cell. It didn't look like anything special, but I saw handwriting on it. It was a simply written note with a Scripture cited and scribbled across it:

> *Peter was therefore kept in prison, but constant prayer was offered to God for him by the church. And when Herod was about to bring him out, that night Peter was sleeping, bound with two chains between two soldiers; and the guards before the door were keeping the prison. Now behold, an angel of the Lord stood by him, and a light shone in the prison; and he struck Peter on the side and raised him up, saying, "Arise quickly!" And his chains fell off his hands. Then the angel said to him, "Gird yourself and tie on your sandals"; and so he did. And he said to him, "Put on your garment and follow me." So he went out and followed him... (Acts 12:5-9 NKJV).*

I never understood the reality of the story until that moment. It seems most of my Christian life had been spent knowing stories without ever allowing God to bring into my life the kind of love and power they revealed. Now, here I was, needing His miraculous power to help me take another step. I thought I had this place figured out the first time, but obviously, somewhere along the line I had become deceived yet again.

I thought about Peter's story and found hope in this: If Peter's captivity in the Book of Acts was as real as what I was experiencing (and what I had experienced earlier), then his supernatural release must have been real, too. I have always believed that what God does for one, He wants to do for many. So I recounted the story of what God did for Peter and asked for God's help, praying: "Dear Lord, please help me to see, help me to believe, to receive from You whatever release You would grant me, and please help me to understand whatever it was You did that day for Peter."

The part of Peter's story that always seems the most striking to me is the constant prayer his fellow believers offered on his behalf. I knew the prayers of others were out of my hands; I could only hope and pray that my friends, family, and co-workers were doing the same for me at that moment. I had to focus on the Lord and the steps that He empowered me to take.

I knew Peter was bound by chains, a condition now becoming all too familiar to me. I realized (perhaps more than I wanted to), how many ways I had been bound—sadly, without even knowing it. I knew that Peter was asleep in the Acts 12 account, and that he was guarded by soldiers inside and out.

Despite it all—and through it all—an angel of the Lord stood by Peter. This was incredible to me; it gave me hope for my own struggles. What a reminder that the Lord is always with us and never leaves our side, even in the most trying of times! That God would send guardian or warring angels to stand beside us speaks to me of His utmost care and commitment. Whether there are angels here with me now or not, I know God is present all around, and for that I am thankful.

ENTER THE LIGHT

Caught up in my thoughts and reasoning, I realized that something was different. Light flooded the room all around me, overpowering the dark. It wasn't a physical light seen with the eyes; instead, this light flooded my heart. But no matter where it was, the light was true and it threw crushing blows against the enemy's attempts at deception.

I already felt more alive as I sought to gaze at the Lord. More light seemed to follow. My chains were gone, and though I was still held captive from His path, I had the strength and energy to embrace His light and use it as a springboard for my release. I knew about the power that lay ahead on His path just outside the prison, and I was determined not to miss out on His plans.

I jumped to my feet quickly, just as Peter had done. I looked up toward the Lord; as I did, I found the rest of Peter's story of release illuminated in my heart and mind. At that moment, I truly understood why the Lord urges us to hide His Word in our hearts: it is for times like this when He brings it back, both to our understanding and for it to become our reality.

The command given Peter by the angel of the Lord was clear: He was to gird himself and to tie on his sandals. He was to put on his garment and follow the angel out of the cell. I could not help but believe that the instructions given to release Peter from his dark place contained a powerful message now sent directly to me.

The angel's first command—*"gird yourself"*—may be the most profound part of what he said. Although Peter's cell was real, I had learned that my captivity was a place of deception. What better way to counter the lies than to gird myself with truth? It is exactly what we are urged to do daily when we put on the armor of God (see Eph. 6:14-17).

If the light of His truth weren't holding me up, the lies of darkness would rebuild my cell and bind me again. At least, that is what I had seen happen before. The enemy has his own set of "truths" that are actually lies, according to God's perspective. He mortars his "truths" together with the circumstances of our lives until they give the appearance of foundational walls we can trust in. Instead of the walls being trustworthy, however, we allow them to define our limits.

It was clear that my truth wasn't enough anymore; I needed God's truth to become mine. "Lord, please gird me up with Your truth."

The Lord was speaking to me and teaching me in new ways. "Reality" was starting to have a whole new spin and perspective. The intensity of the experience caused an overload of sorts. Still, I knew I had to persevere, battle, and step forward to get out of this place again—hopefully for the last time. I was sick and tired of captivity, yet I knew that the Lord was teaching me how to keep my focus on Him.

For that, I am thankful.

GETTING "DRESSED"

Despite the great importance the Lord impressed upon my heart to gird myself with His truth and not my own, I knew there was more, much more. The second command Peter received from the angel was: *"tie on your sandals."* Seeing as I was wearing running shoes, I knew this too was a figurative lesson I needed to understand.

Just as I had pondered the idea of truth, I thought about the armor of God and the fact that God wants our feet to be fitted with the Gospel of peace (see Eph. 6:15). I knew this to mean one thing: Peace was to be the path for my steps. I had to resist the fears that came with this place in life and I had to deny my own anxieties; I had to step forward in the perfect peace that surpasses my understanding and circumstances. Softly, I heard whispered through my soul, "I will keep you in perfect peace because your mind is stayed on Me, because you trust in Me" (see Isa. 26:3).

I can't say I know what was really going on with Peter, but I was beginning to understand that God wanted me to strap on something more than sandals. I had to embrace His supernatural peace that comes only from focusing intently on Him. It was amazing to hear the Lord so simply in my heart; it was even more amazing not to be surprised by it anymore. I was starting to expect this kind of intimacy and power of God in and around my life. It was this place of abiding in Him that brought me the greatest peace and strength I had ever known.

But I was still in the place of captivity.

The last thing that I remember Peter doing before being released from his cell was putting on his garment. Personally, I always relate the word *garment* to the psalms; I think of putting on a garment of praise and thanksgiving. And I believe this is where the Lord was leading me.

I can only imagine how Peter must have felt being unfairly locked up in that prison cell. He had served the Lord with the best of intentions. Yet for his trouble, he was afflicted with unpleasant circumstances all around him. It reminds me of the bitterness I felt when I first woke up on the cold, hard floor of my prison. It felt dark, limiting, and unfair. I've experienced in my life and watched in others' lives times when bitterness snowballed and became big enough to affect every thought and perception. It is in those times that I've seen bitterness change my perception of truth the most.

From all this, I knew this garment of praise and thanksgiving was one I had to wear every day. It would keep me looking up at

Him instead of at self. It would keep me trusting His ways and methods and would therefore keep me thankful for God's ability to deliver in any and all circumstances. Praise and thanksgiving would keep me from growing bitter. Praise had helped me leave the prison the first time; it could only help me to leave it again, because praise transforms my perspective.

Yet nothing happened. I had surrendered my truth for God's truth. I had overcome fear to put on the shoes of peace. I had adorned myself with praises to Him, even though my outer circumstances did not look good. Still, I was right in the middle of utter darkness. Enough was enough! I knew I could not allow the enemy to hold me captive from the Lord's path and purposes any longer. I closed my eyes and stepped forward…

Like stepping into a pool in the middle of the desert, I was instantly on a whole new path, out of my prison and released to walk forward again toward Him. Left behind were the lies I once thought of as truth, the fears I allowed to paralyze me, and the bitter circumstances I allowed to beat me down. They could go with me no longer; I had to move forward to join the Lord. I just had to step, step toward the Lord. Before I even put my foot down on the path, I saw the Lord, and He was already stepping toward me.

I had to let go of control and trust Him. Then He whisked me away.

Chapter 7

THE VISION

THE LORD AND I stood on a ledge before a long, downward grassy hill. The hill rolled forward into a valley that looked nothing like the grass above it. It looked dry, and the sun beat down hard upon it. There were no trees, but plenty of rocks and sand. In the distance I saw that the desert plain gradually rose higher until it reached a peak far away. As the ground rose, it became less sandy and the grass seemed to become more prevalent again.

We started walking, and the Lord spoke: "This land is a model of the journey you will encounter. It is a representation of the different seasons in your life as they flow together for one purpose.

"First we stood on ground that seemed normal to both your eyes and your footsteps. It is a place of familiarity from which I am calling you to step forward. We stepped together and are now walking down this grassy hill. Do not look ahead again to the dry valley. Your eyes will reveal it to you if you focus on it, but I want you present in this moment with Me. Look only to Me, and I will sustain you where you need to be right now. We are going downhill and there is no resistance to your steps. In fact, you are rolling with the hill and are being guided by Me.

"This hill is the time to receive. This is why you cannot look to the future. If you focus on what is ahead, then you will miss out on what I want to give you now. This is the time I am filling you up. I am teaching you and will stretch your thoughts and heart beyond where they have been previously. I will strengthen you, and I—I repeat, *I*—will prepare you. You cannot prepare yourself for the next season. You must trust Me.

"Our time moving down this hill together will go by the fastest, because the momentum of My Spirit is carrying you. Do not miss out on resting with Me in intimacy, for it is the only water that will satisfy and nourish you for your next steps. Do not lose sight of Me. Most of all, I want you to enjoy Me and enjoy our closeness together. I know I do.

"Look, we are now in the valley."

I looked down and noticed there was no longer grass between my toes; it was now sand. I looked behind us and realized we had been down here for a long time already. I had spent so much time seeking Him and His presence that He had carried me through much of the dry heat of the valley. I had not even noticed. We were already more than halfway to where the ground started to elevate.

"Keep drinking of Me, My child. Do you see that when you do not focus on the circumstances around you, they cannot inflict pain? You were so caught up in Me that you didn't even know you were in a painful or difficult place. Does this show you where you must keep your eyes?

"This valley will not keep you and will only make you stronger. No matter how hot it gets or how thirsty you are, do not be afraid to stop with Me. It will be tempting to press forward to get through faster, but this will only prolong your time here. Remember that I have you here for a reason. You will stay in the valley until you have received what I want to give you in the valley. Don't miss out on it, for it is an opportunity to set up camp with Me. We can share incredible times together."

I looked up again to find that suddenly, we were at the middle of the hill and still going up. The rocky terrain hurt my feet. I felt the Lord's hand still locked with mine, but at the same time I saw Him at the top of the hill. To know that He was not only with me, but also ahead of me, gave me tremendous hope and perseverance for each step.

There were more obstacles here than at any other part of the journey that I had seen. It was not nearly as hot, but the sun was still scorching. It was nice to be out of the sand, but the climb was tiring. It was too bright to see Him next to me so I had to believe. I held onto my faith, believing that it was His hand still grasping mine, even while it was He who waited for me at the top of the hill.

APPROACHING THE VISION

I reached the mount's peak, which stemmed up from the valley, and fell into His arms. He welcomed my embrace but lifted me to see what He saw. Far off in the distance, there was a light at the top of a steep plateau like none I had ever seen before. There was a celebration booming just within the light's source. I knew it was something He wanted me to see, like a spark of His light ahead. I could not make out the details but I knew it was there. I believed Him. I believed that the Lord truly had a purpose for my life and was walking me toward it. I could not wait to get there, but I knew I would have to.

"You're right!" He exclaimed. "This is a glimpse of the vision that I have ahead for you. I want you to see it so you will believe. Many trying times are coming soon, and you will have to trust Me in order to stay the course. Believe Me when I tell you that I will take you there if you will surrender control, obey My voice, and trust Me. You must see that great things lie ahead so that you will not lose hope in faith. Be careful, though. Do not trust in the vision; you must only trust in Me. I have many great things planned in your life and that vision ahead is just one of them. Please do not let anything cause you to miss out on Me.

"We are about to move on so you will get an idea of what the rest of your journey includes. As you walk, I want you to remember one thing, if nothing else: Only I can place you in the vision I have cast for your life. You cannot walk there on your own. It is not something you can plan, nor is it something you can achieve. But if you will remain in Me each day and keep your eyes on Me, you will find yourself there before you know it and in ways you could not even imagine.

"I will bring adversity on all flesh, but I will give your life to you as a prize in all places, wherever you go. Those I have used in mighty ways could not have conjured up the ways in which I fulfilled their purposes. Joseph could not have imagined that placing himself in prison would serve to fulfill the calling on his life. Daniel would not have chosen a den of lions as his path. But I will take you there if you will let go and trust Me."

We walked forward, and the Lord continued speaking. "As I said before, things will not be easy on this path, especially if you are walking it by faith. No matter what circumstances you face or what people say, you must listen to My Living Word and trust what I have told you. I will place you in this vision, probably when you least expect it—and I will do it by means that you would not think to use."

As we started to descend the mountain, I noticed immediately that I had to be careful with each step. I began asking the Lord for advice, even in the little things. More often than not, I even had to ask Him where I should plant my foot and on which rock I should step. The terrain was jagged in places and didn't allow for a smooth walk down. Every time I asked Him a question, He answered me in some way or another, but I could only hear His answer when my eyes were on Him.

The farther we walked back toward the valley, the higher the plateau before us seemed to rise. That was where the vision was. It wasn't right at the top or on the edge, but a distance ahead of us. I couldn't tell how far away it was. I was tempted to wonder how I could ever get up there. But the Lord had ingrained in me the fact that only He could put me there. From where I stood, it certainly looked like He was right.

The circumstances grew more difficult upon our descent and made it hard to even walk. I tried to believe Him, because nothing I saw made any sense. Yet I knew what He had called me to and I knew I had to be obedient. We reached the valley again, but it didn't stretch very far before the plateau took over.

I walked into the valley and sat down quietly. The plateau was overwhelming. There was no physical way to climb it. It was kind of depressing and I was very tired. I couldn't handle much more. I wanted to believe the Lord, but it was growing more difficult to trust.

The Lord stood at the base of the plateau and said, "Keep walking, just one step at a time. I have given you the strength and wisdom to do it."

I locked my eyes upon the Lord and took a step. Then I took another, and another. "Wait! Stay right there, My child. I love you."

"Lord, it's OK. I feel strong enough, I want to step out. I was coming over to You. I know You will help me climb the plateau."

"I have asked you to wait," the Lord replied. "This is where you are to be. Though I love your faith, it's not time to take another step; it is time to make camp together, right here."

TIME TO WAIT

I couldn't believe my ears. I thought it was time to move. I trusted that He could overcome and believed that He would. I didn't think I could handle just sitting and waiting. It felt like it required more strength to wait than to step forward. But I knew I had to heed His voice, so I calmed down and settled in.

We had been there for what must have been half a day, but I hardly noticed. Our time together was amazing. The Lord spoke to me and taught me for hours. We worshiped together and spent a long time in prayer, even silent prayer. It was one of the richest times I had ever spent with anyone. I forgot all about where we were and about the task ahead. Praying for others helped me take my eyes off myself. Seeking Him became all-consuming. I stood up to stretch and felt a gentle breeze. The breeze kept coming and grew stronger. The Lord lifted me into His arms and suddenly, we rode the winds upward.

We scaled the plateau and were now headed for the top. I let out a sigh of relief because I knew He was doing just what He said He would—and in His perfect timing. I'm so glad He instructed me to wait; it was as though in that short time, He had given me wings. He carried me up toward the path and vision He had shown me, and then positioned me as only He could. I rested in Him and began to fall asleep.

Chapter 8

HIDDEN TREASURES

I COULDN'T REMEMBER MUCH from the model the Lord had just shown me, yet I knew that my heart had recorded every word and experience. The only thing I could remember was the vision ahead and the beauty it held for me. I knew that I would someday be there in His timing if I could give up control and trust Him alone. The vision gave me hope that I did indeed have a purpose. It helped me understand that there is a vision for everyone. It is waiting to be found and we are to help others find theirs. That is what the blessing is all about: offering His life by helping others to see His vision.

My experience at the garage sale had taken a lot out of me. I could feel the warfare from the enemy even though I knew I was safe in the Lord's arms. It can be very hard to let go of control and trust Him whom we cannot physically see. But being very close to Him brought a strong peace, no matter where we were. I didn't know where we were going, and I probably didn't need to know. I didn't want to breathe without Him. I had never felt this way about the Lord. The closer we came together, the closer I wanted to be.

The Lord used the garage sale to show me the façades of the enemy more clearly. Now, every step we took allowed me to understand more about how we keep ourselves captive and thus prevent ourselves from receiving.

DEEP IN HIS LOVE

The Lord had me in awe of Him. His true and unconditional love for me was clearer than ever. The more I received His love for me, the more I loved Him. I didn't have words to describe it.

Jesus truly is the lover of our souls. I wanted never to leave this new place of intimacy with Him. I wanted my heart to beat with His. He really means for us to have a flourishing love relationship with Him. I had missed out on more of it than I cared to know, in part because I had never realized how blind I could be to things that weren't right inside my own little world.

This increasing intimacy with the Lord gave my life more direction than any class, person, or experience ever had before. I sensed that this oneness with Him was essential for the journey that lay ahead.

The longer we walked together, the more I tried to sit still and soak up what only His presence could provide. I found out that true intimacy with Him really does transform us. I yearned to know the Lord's thoughts and ways. I couldn't help but want to worship Him. But even as I worshiped, I failed to find words that would suffice. I wanted to bless His heart, but I didn't know how. I looked directly at Him and cried from my heart to learn how to worship Him fully.

My sense of smell distracted me as I became aware of the sweetest, most desirable fragrance I'd ever encountered. We seemed to be heading toward the source of the scent; with each step, it got stronger. We came to a stop in front of a small, homely shack. I couldn't imagine how such a beautiful smell could come from a place like this. But the aroma was so strong that I ached to understand it. There was a sign over the door of the shack with a long inscription:

> *A time is coming and has now come when the true worshipers will worship the Father in spirit and truth, for they are the kind of worshipers the Father seeks* (John 4:23).

The Lord set me down on my feet but didn't let go of my hand. He knocked on the door, and we waited for the answer. I became curious. The Lord's face took on a glow of anticipation as we awaited the person inside. I wondered who it was that touched His heart so deeply. Just then, the door opened and the breeze covered us with the incredible scent. A woman stood in the doorway and the Lord embraced her.

He looked at me with a smile. "This is My dear child, Mary Magdalene," He said. "She is a true worshiper."

My heart nearly stopped from the love this woman gave to her Lord. Mary had learned what it meant to worship and move the heart of God. The two of them talked while I mostly listened. "That's where the fragrance is coming from," I recalled out loud.

THE FRAGRANCE OF WORSHIP

Now I remembered why the scent was so exquisite and powerful: it was the lingering fragrance of the worship displayed in the actions and sacrifice of Mary's life. Most notably, it came from the perfume which she'd broken open to anoint the Lord days before His death on the cross. She let down her hair that day and used it to wipe away the dirt from her Lord's feet (see Luke 7:38). Her worship was unconventional and was questioned by others; yet it was this unmeasured sacrifice that brought her worship to life.

"Mary," I asked, "how did you know how to worship the Lord in such a way? I struggle to find words or actions that seem sufficient."

Jesus glanced at us both. "Mary's worship went far beyond words or even the mind's comprehension. She held back nothing from Me. It didn't matter to her what others thought. She let go of herself and latched onto Me no matter what the cost. She worshiped Me with all that she was because she loved Me with all that she was. Such worship cannot be measured in mere words, but must be lived out in all of your life."

Mary smiled sheepishly, and I knew we needed to move on. The Lord loved it here. Her life was worship that kept on singing.

Their good-bye was only temporary. She knew what it was to abide in the Lord always and would be back with Him repeatedly. I wanted what she had with Jesus. To be complete, I *needed* what she had.

"You're more than welcome," He blurted out in response to my deep thanks.

I wanted to walk out the life of a worshiper. Back in His arms, I dozed off muttering prayers to know Him more. What a treasure it was to be still in His presence! This realization crystallized more and more as His Spirit ministered to me in ways I had never known before.

LEARNING TO WALK

Our journey moved forward and I awoke from my nap completely rejuvenated. I glanced around and saw that our environment was changing from a dry wilderness to the beginning of something new. The season was also changing to what looked like spring.

We were somewhere *very* new. Our intimacy had grown even closer since our visit with Mary. I had been released from the prison of living within myself, and freed to live in Him. What greater freedom could I ever desire?

The Lord stopped us suddenly. "It's here you must learn to walk again. Even though it will be you that is walking, you will not be walking on your own. You will be fine as long as you do not stray from My voice. I will stay with you to the extent that you abide in Me. Draw near to Me, and I will draw near to you."[1]

He stood me on my feet and continued on. "You can be in My arms whenever you so desire. I will continue to lead you in the proper direction for as long as you will listen to Me. Your eyes are better now, aren't they? The longer you remain focused on Me, the more you are enabled to see. As we continue forward, you must not lose this focus. Follow Me. Pursue Me."

I walked with the Lord but it felt like I was being carried. My vision was much clearer and I saw things in a new light. I was walking again on my own legs, but it was much different from before. There was new strength coming from outside of me.

"You are learning to let My grace be your steps. A large part of the grace you walk in each day comes from the prayers of those around you. The prayers of others carry you through much more than you'll ever know. As long as you allow yourself to receive from Me, I will be your strength. You must abide in Me in every moment, no matter what the circumstances might bring.

"Your vision will continue to increase the longer your focus remains on me. You must not let your own eyes lead you when walking through tough times. What they tell you will not be your answer. I will remind you again to seek My voice and look at Me. I will lead you through your answer."

I had tremendous hope for what was ahead; it contained such light, and I knew it was from Him. I couldn't focus too hard on it, because doing so would put me in danger of missing our current step. I knew I had to be careful not to stay in the past, nor focus too much on the light ahead. Focusing behind or ahead would mean missing out on where the Father was moving and where I was to join Him.

JUDGMENT'S WAR CRY

Suddenly, loud noises from just over the hill began ringing in my ears. They were the loud cries of men, women, boys, and girls. Each cry seemed to be filled with different emotions. I heard sounds of fear, anguish, and anger, all of which blended into the sound of a war. The cries got louder as we reached the top of the grassy hill. From the peak, I could see the source of the yelling. Something horrendous was happening.

When my eyes took in the view of those standing in the valley below us, my heart sank. I knew exactly who these people were. They were prisoners—captives to themselves. They weren't fully surrounded by prison cells with bars and walls, but they were draped with the chains of judgment.

A dark cloud hovered above the valley our hilltop overlooked. The cloud blocked the light that was all around us. It was enough to squash and discourage any true love the people might otherwise have for one another.

The Lord motioned me to join Him as He walked toward the group. The closer we came to them, the more I believed that they didn't recognize their chains or realize that what they were doing to one another was so detrimental. It had become too much a part of their lives.

We reached the darkened group, which numbered somewhere in the hundreds. Their cries grew deeper and more difficult to bear. I don't think they saw the pain they inflicted on one another. Each loosed his or her own chains just long enough to strike—and literally bludgeon—someone else. The cloud that lingered over the people was a cloud of condemnation. They did not know it, but they were bringing their pain and oppression upon themselves. Their pride and insecurities were sharpened knives used to dig into the hearts of others and ruin them.

Judgment hides itself so that it can come out in full force. I could see the Lord's pain drip from His eyes. "Go closer. Take a look at each of them and tell me what you see," He said.

I stepped further into the mob and saw Bibles flying through the air. The Bibles were being used as a means of attack. I recognized the people to be Christians; some of them were church leaders. They were using truth, but without offering grace.

A Bible struck a woman next to me, and she fell to her knees in chains. I was disgusted at the thought of those who would do this. I tried to run back to the Lord, but before I could get going, I fell to the ground. I wiggled away from the crowd until I was at His feet. As I looked down, I saw a chain binding my feet.

"I went there, Lord, and they bound me. Who are they?" I asked.

With a soft look of love, He turned to me. "They're your brothers and sisters in Me. They didn't put that chain on your feet. You did."

I was confused until He explained. "When you saw how judgment bound them, you also began to judge them. I did not show you these people and their sin so that you would add to the condemnation already plaguing them. It is an easy trap to fall into and a hard one to resist.

"When I show you something, it is not so you can judge the person. I show you these things so you will begin to pray for and love them. You have received a new vision and you are able to see much more than you once could. But you must use this vision to look for Me in each of their hearts. You must see the treasures and potential that emanate from My place in their lives."

Convicted, I begged for forgiveness. With a smile, He directed me. "Go into the crowd again, then come and tell me what you really see."

I tried not to look at the outer appearance of the group or even their actions. I focused on one particular individual. A young boy had sat down in the center of the commotion, so I began to watch him and pray on his behalf.

Every now and then a smile broke forth. My prayers for him intensified. I began to develop a love for this young man. I didn't even know him, but the more I lifted his heart to the Lord in prayer the more I loved him. I saw him in a much different light now. I was trying to see him the way the Lord had taught me to—through His eyes.

There was a unique beauty in the boy's heart. I got excited about what I saw, so I looked to another person whom I could love in prayer. I realized that within each person, there were different but wonderful treasures that could only be seen through love. Watching and praying in this way allowed me to see in others the potential I believe the Lord sees in each of us.

As I left the crowd I was encouraged. I understood that we each are the ones called to break the cycle of judgment. That is why the chain bound me at first. If I focused on what others were doing wrong I would only add to the condemnation. But if I blessed and focused on what was right about each person, then maybe all of us could join together in leaving our chains behind.

The experience was invaluable. I so badly wanted to learn to see everyone in this new way. Jesus looked to me and smiled.

"Let's go. There is much ahead."

TREASURES IN HEAVEN

The green, grassy fields through which we had been traveling now collided with a large, beautiful structure built of trees and bushes. Its appearance was so beautiful that little else could stand in comparison.

"It's time," the Lord stated. "Come with Me inside. There is a lot I want to show you."

The Lord entered the structure and guided me with His hand. The light was brighter than any I had ever seen. It was almost overwhelming, but at the same time it was soothing. As my eyes adjusted, I could take in all that surrounded me.

"Go ahead," He suggested. "Look around."

My heart nearly skipped a beat. The structure was made of trees, bushes, and vines. They were all very full and thick, and their height stretched toward the heavens. The greens surrounding us were overshadowed by the fruit they bore. Everywhere I looked

I saw large, plump fruit. There was no earthly comparison to what grew here. The colors and shapes varied and none of it was old or rotten.

I looked over at the Lord, and He smiled. "Do you like it? This is the fruit of My Spirit.[2] This is one of the many things I want My children to partake of. This is fruit that remains.[3] Each piece is waiting to be picked and purposed. I AM the vine and you are the branches.[4] This is the fruit that I am bringing forth. Will you bear it?"

The Lord finished speaking, and I continued to glance around. I saw a rare break in the barrage of greenery, so I went to investigate it.

"I was waiting for you to find this," He responded. I looked up and couldn't help but notice a large board that stretched out far across the structure in each direction. There were a few randomly scattered puzzle pieces that stood unconnected to each other placed here and there. I looked down to find another intriguing discovery: a large, somewhat dusty, heart-shaped treasure chest. Fingerprints marked its edges in a few places. It was obviously very old and was far underused. I looked over to the Lord with a curious expression.

"Go ahead and open it," the Lord urged me.

My hands fought off the dust. I lifted the lid of the giant heart, hoping to find gold and silver treasures inside. I was very surprised to find piles upon piles of glowing puzzle pieces. I wondered whether they were the same as those randomly scattered on the board above.

All of the pieces shone, each with its own unique reflection. Each had a picture that was difficult to see through the glare. I sorted through the chest, piece by piece, but still couldn't see what the pieces depicted. Surely, they had to represent more than they appeared to show. If there was one thing I was learning, it was the fact that, with the Lord, everything was more than what it appeared to be.

Finally, the Lord reached down, grabbed a piece, and placed it in my hand, saying, "Look at this piece in the proper light and tell me what is there."

I continued to struggle with the glare until finally, I caught the right light. I tilted the piece until it faced Jesus. It was then that I could see the picture in the puzzle piece: It was an image of me and of what the Lord was doing in my life. More specifically, it was a representation of His presence in and through my life—a picture of my heart and His purpose for me, as He saw them.

I shuffled through the pieces as the Lord reached out to hand me another one. This time I pointed it directly toward Him so that the reflection came from His light rather than from our surroundings. The piece revealed the image of Christ, just as my own piece had. I also saw the young boy from the rioting crowd—the boy for whom I had just prayed. Much of what the Lord had shown me was now reflected from within the piece. I saw many of the same treasures in his heart that the Lord had shown me when I looked upon this boy in the crowd of people just before.

The Lord picked up one piece after another, looking at each one with intense love. As He looked, His eyes drew out the treasures in each one.

"Here," said the Lord. "Lift your piece up to Me, and I will place it within My Father's plan. Each person who will receive that which I have released them to and will abide in Me to the fullest will be brought here. I wait for all of My children to understand their piece and their purpose in Me. My children have within them so many treasures that languish and become covered by dust.

"I can't emphasize it enough: I long for all of My children to find their treasures and their purpose in Me. Then they can put their puzzle pieces back in My hand and I will place them within My Father's plan, just as I am now doing with your piece. That is when the pieces will begin to connect and reveal the full picture of what is yet to be.

"Each of you is a different piece of Me and of My Father's plan. You have to continue to learn to see in others and in yourselves the treasures of the heart. This chest is full of treasures, but you must look through My eyes to see them. These treasures are what I am asking you to bless in others. Bless them so they can see these treasures for themselves. These are treasures that neither moth nor rust will destroy, because they are your treasures in Heaven.[5] These treasures can only be found in Me."

I gave my piece to the Lord and He placed it perfectly within the puzzle as only He knew how. I was amazed at how few of the pieces were in place and how many were yet to be fitted into the picture. I was so humbled to be in this place with Him— humbled by His presence, by His perfect plan, and by the self-imposed captivity that had kept me from joining Him here for so long.

He knew what I was thinking and said, "Be thankful that you are here now. I forgive you for the sins that have kept you from this place. Please continue to meet Me here so you don't miss out on where we are going. Our intimacy together will always be your path back here. As the vine and the branches we must be grafted together. You cannot miss what is ahead."

I nodded my head and began to walk with Him. We moved to exit the place, but stopped. "This place—" He said, "—now that I have shown it to you, please bring others here."

My heart was a little heavy from all that I had taken in, but I was still very encouraged by it all. The Lord's arm rested around me as we headed toward a door. I decided to stop, and stood still for a moment. The Lord looked at me warmly. "What is it?" He asked.

"Lord, can we sit for a little while? I need more time just being still with You. I need it if I am to continue on."

His answer was clear, even without speaking. His face lit up, and He said, "Of course we can. I was just waiting for you to stop and ask Me."

Chapter 9

THE RED SEA

"LORD, I'M READY TO go when You are."

The Lord stood up and drew me near. His hands invited me to walk forward from this fruitful place. Being together had made this one of the greatest moments of my life—so much so that I didn't want to leave. He had ministered to me in ways I didn't understand or know enough to ask for. I felt reenergized. I was amazed, too, at how much the Lord cherished our intimate time together. I had no idea it meant that much to Him

Yet I knew it was time to go. The ivy corridor that surrounded our exit was budding with life. The path was very narrow and was becoming even more difficult to follow. Ahead of us, at the end of the path, stood a gate that was illumined by the glory of the Lord. I looked into His face as eager questions lined up in my heart. He looked at me with a smile and reached for my hand. I got the sense that He was urging me to trust Him.

Our steps reached the gate and we came to a halt. "Knock," He said, "and it will be opened to you."[1] I knocked on the gate gently. It opened without resistance and seemed to readily invite our passage.

The light was still strong, but our next step led us into a full, thick fog that troubled my eyes. I stopped walking to look ahead.

"Why are you looking with your eyes?" He asked. "You have to trust where I have directed your heart. There is no place for worry here. Abide in Me and trust My voice. Come on, you must continue to walk. You must take this journey one step at a time and join Me with every step. Remain in Me and inquire of Me before you move and you will know wisdom for your path. My plan is perfect and My grace will always bring you back to it if you will allow. Do not forget, you can only walk as far as you have allowed My grace to precede you."

I did as He said and walked one step at a time. With every step I began to understand how much I needed His wisdom in even the tiniest details. The fog was still thick and I couldn't see beyond the place where I stood. The Lord's peace still held me steady. I got the impression that there was something incredible ahead. I couldn't wait to see where we were going. I wanted to prepare myself for it.

"It is neither your duty nor your responsibility to prepare yourself for what I'm calling you to," the Lord stated in response to my thoughts. "Only I can prepare your heart properly. My ways are not your ways and My thoughts are not your thoughts.[2] If you knew what lay ahead, it is likely that you would do more damage to yourself than good. You would react to and depend on your prior knowledge and understanding rather than depending on My voice. You must bind yourself to Me and allow Me to be your eyes, ears, thoughts, words, and all your senses. To walk where I desire to take you, it must be remembered that it is no longer you who live, but it is I who live in and through you."[3]

I took another step and stopped. I reached for the ground ahead of me and felt what seemed to be grass grazing my hand. I stretched my leg forward to take a step and fell immediately. My breathing nearly stopped as I grabbed the edge of the cliff to halt my descent. The flow of panic seemed to displace the flow of my blood. Then I felt the Lord's hands wrap around mine. He had never left me. He pulled me up and set me down to gather myself together.

THE "LETTING GO" LESSON

"Lord, what happened? I put my hand down and felt what I knew to be solid ground. Why didn't You warn me?"

"You didn't allow Me to. You became so confident in your own ability to discern what was coming that you trusted in those feelings instead of Me. Please remember that in the days ahead things will not always be as they seem. I will never leave you or forsake you,[4] but it is possible for you to create more pain than necessary when you fail to listen to My voice. I had to allow you to make this mistake because there was much that you needed to learn. In these days ahead, each of you will be called to walk by faith, not by sight."[5]

I processed His wisdom, realizing that although I had always known this truth, I had never truly lived it. What does it really mean to walk by faith instead of sight?

"Jump," He said. "It's time."

"*What?* I just fell and had to be rescued, and now You want me to jump. Lord, I don't know if I can do it."

"I'm not asking you whether you can; I'm asking if you *will*. It wasn't the right time before, but now you must trust My timing and take this leap of faith. You can't have faith until you decide to walk in it. You must choose faith with actions if you wish to truly know faith" (see James 2:20).

I didn't want to jump, but I knew I had to trust the Lord and all that He spoke to me. "Don't worry," He offered. "Just go."

I tiptoed to the edge and plunged into thin air from the high place where I stood, preparing for a long fall. My whole body slammed into the ground.

"Ouch, that hurt!" I exclaimed. "But You told me—"

"Precisely," said the Lord. "I'm sorry the ground caused you pain, but your faith must be tested in order to build its strength in Me. Obedience will sometimes hurt, but you must trust Me through those times. I will never take you through more than you can handle[6] and am always working all things together for good.[7]

"Following Me won't always be comfortable or painless, but you have to trust Me regardless of how the circumstances look. Continue to persevere no matter what. Perseverance comes only as you continue to walk by faith, find hope in Me, and allow our love to be the strength of your life."

Considering these recent steps and experiences, I stopped trying to predict and plan what might be ahead. I wanted so badly to step out in faith again, but I waited for the Lord's voice to direct me.

What He said next encouraged me: "Know this: My Father and I are very proud of you. We love you so very much. Never let the enemy trick you into believing that the circumstances you are being taken through mean that you are loved less. Rather, know that these trying times that require such faith are but a testament to how much I do indeed love you. You will need to be prepared for the days ahead. These hardships are preparing you. You are learning how to lean on Me instead of on yourself or others. My Father loves you as He has loved Me."

I let out a great sigh. I needed to hear that. I knew that He had been sharing that love with me daily, but I also realized that I would need to take more time to listen to what He wanted to share. He is always speaking, but I must quiet myself and listen.

"Are you ready?" He asked.

"Ready for what?" I answered cautiously.

"It's time to walk again. Will you jump when I tell you to?"

I wanted to hesitate. I was still sore from the last time. Instead, I nodded, knowing that it would be worth paying any price for what the Lord had ahead. I could still see the light of His glory glimmering in the fog. I looked to Him one last time and then jumped. As I flew from my feet, I felt amazingly free and found the freedom comforting.

I was, in fact, falling into His plan. My sight was still limited, but wherever I looked, I saw the hand of God wrapped completely around me. I was truly in the palm of His hand and enjoying every moment. He had carried me so many times before in my life, but I had taken the pleasure for granted. Now, as I hurtled deeper into this plunge of faith, things became clearer. With every step of faith my vision increased; every bit of faith I chose to walk in produced more sight. I stopped striving to see and decided to trust where He was taking me.

SEA OF GRACE

Before I knew it, my feet were entrenched in sand and I stood next to the Lord on a beach. The fog still blurred my sight, but even more of His glory shone all around.

I quickly embraced my Savior with a hug. "Thank You for helping me to jump. I was nervous, but once I obeyed Your voice I felt an unbelievable freedom."

The Lord smiled at me and chuckled. "There is great freedom just waiting to be enjoyed, but it requires those leaps of faith. Your vision has improved because you walked by faith and not by sight. Your eyes will limit you, but true faith will give you freedom to see.

"Your vision has improved, and that is a great gift. The problem begins when you try to use the gift on your own. My weaknesses are still many times stronger than even your greatest strengths. This is why you must continue to let Me be your sight. I am the only sight that will never fail you.

"It is this way for all of your gifts. Don't abandon the gifts I have given you, but offer them up to Me. No doubt I will use them. You will not have to strive. If you will focus on Me, your gifts will come naturally and be a part of your life. Dependence on Me is not designed just for times of weakness, but for every moment of your life. If you stop listening for My voice, you will have placed yourself in danger of starting your own path."

We continued walking through the sand until we were near the shoreline and I could hear the sound of waves before us. Two or three steps more and He led us to a body of water unlike any I had ever seen. The fog gently rested over this ocean, and I beheld an unparalleled sight. The body of water at our feet was bright red. I rubbed my eyes to check myself and looked again. The water's color was confirmed.

"Is this the Red Sea?" I asked.

"It is, but it is not the one you are thinking of."

"What are we doing here? Are we going somewhere else? Are You going to part the waters?"

"No," He responded. "We are going to cross it. Much awaits you there."

"But how are we going to cross? It's an ocean. I know I can't swim that far."

The Lord looked at me and gripped me with His eyes. "We'll walk, just as we have been walking. The sea is water only according to your sight. This sea is actually My grace. You must walk upon My grace to go where I have called you—and the only way to walk on it is by faith.

"This is the real Red Sea. It is My blood. My blood is both the grace and the freedom I have given to you to live by. To walk in My purposes in the times that are ahead, you must understand that My grace is the only foundation upon which your feet can rest. That is why faith is so vital."

He looked at me and asked, "Are you ready?"

I wondered what it would be like to walk with Him here and realized that this wasn't just a step of faith, but a walk of faith.

"The world will try to convince you that many things are impossible, but remember that with Me all things are possible."[8]

My eye spotted the image of a man standing some 20 yards away on the water. He looked at me as though he knew exactly who I was. He flashed a wide smile and waved his arms to motion me forward.

The Lord looked at the man and laughed. "You can see that Peter has finally gotten past his fears and disbelief."

"What?" I asked. "That's Peter—Simon Peter—Your friend and disciple? The same Peter You called out of the boat and onto the waters?"

"So you do know that it's possible," He said. "Peter fought the same battles of unbelief you are fighting now. He has overcome his fears and has countered them with trust and faith. He eventually placed his trust in My love.

"Perfect love casts out all fear when you live believing that My love for you is perfect.[9] When you know that I love you perfectly, what is there to fear? Now Peter is able to help others to the place that I helped him reach. You will soon be able to do the same. Trust Me for that first step and keep your eyes upon Me instead of what the world and others are telling you. If you truly follow me, what need is there to see on your own? Remember with whom it is that you are walking. I will always be with you as long and as much as you will allow."

I looked to my feet and again to the sea of His grace. My eyes blinked for an instant as I hesitated before making my decision.

"Here goes!" As I stepped, I looked into the Lord's eyes. A deep and soothing peace washed over me. I felt as though I could soar. My foot stepped upon His grace and I walked where I once thought it was impossible. The Lord grasped my hand firmly, and we walked to join Peter on the waves.

I felt like a child just learning to toddle. I focused on all the promises I knew the Lord had given me, and kept my eyes on Him. With each new step my stride became sturdier and I felt more confident. A wave appeared just ahead of us and was rolling straight into our path. I looked directly at the wave, feeling sure that I could tame it. Before I knew it, I was flattened on the waters and sinking beneath the surface.

"Jesus! Help Lord, please." Before I could finish the sentence, He was already lifting me up. His grace still surrounded us; I was taken aback by the experience, but determined to get up.

Again, I stood on the waters. "Your faith has increased immeasurably, but you have put it in yourself rather than in Me. The strength of one's faith comes from the power of its source. The only source strong enough for you to stand upon is Me. Be careful where you place your faith."

I was very humbled by the incident but thankful for its lesson. The Lord had sent that wave. It was a test to see where I would place my trust and focus. The incident reminded me of the truth that *"God opposes the proud but gives grace to the humble."*[10] I needed to walk upon grace, so my only choice was to live in humility.

"Never stop asking Me for wisdom," the Lord urged me. "The life I have given you is too vital for you to rely on the wisdom of the world."

Peter soon left us, for there were many others he was called to encourage. We didn't really talk, but Peter's example and testimony imparted great volumes of strength and faith into my walk. Knowing that he had prevailed in the same battle that I was facing taught me so much. I learned that through the battle, the Lord helped Peter to release himself from his own unbelief. As a result, he was able to help release me from mine.

MY ONE AND ONLY

Loud voices echoed from afar, but I could not see their source. It sounded as though many were crying out, but in a very joyful way. There didn't seem to be any anguish or hurt in their sound. Instead, their voices were filled with thanksgiving, love, and passion.

A patchy fog still sat before us. I felt as if we had been walking forever. I wondered whether we were ever going to get there.

"Lord? How much longer?"

His spirit seemed grieved over my asking. "Is that why you are with Me? Is it only to get to our destination? Indeed that is where we are going, but are you not content in the journey alone? Is it not enough to simply be with Me?"

He didn't speak angrily, but His eyes told the story. I ached from the pit of my being because I knew I had saddened Him.

"Contentment," He said, "is one of the highest forms of worship. Very little blesses Me more than when one of My children is content with having nothing more than Me. This is one of My greatest desires for each of you—to be totally satisfied with Me alone."

I felt convicted because I knew the truth of His desire. It is so easy to get caught up in the twists and turns of life. I know I miss out on being with Him because I become so focused on doing. I turned and hugged Him as closely as I could as we stood on the waters. I couldn't press myself close enough to Him.

"Lord You are my refuge." I meant it: Every step with the Lord was pure joy. I did not want to miss out on one bit of our time together.

FACE IN THE MIRROR

The fog was heavier now. Visibility was limited to very close range. He was my compass. This went on for quite a while. The light emanating from the Lord shone brightly ahead of us, clearing up much of the fog.

Faint images emerged from the fog ahead, and I realized there were two people walking directly toward us on the waters. My curiosity had already been amplified by our previous encounter on the sea; now it increased with every step that took us nearer to the approaching water-walkers.

As the gap between us closed, I thought about the journey so far and realized that I had already met Paul, Mary, and Peter.

Interrupting my own train of thought, I wondered aloud, "Who is this that we're approaching?"

"This is an encounter you must face in order to walk where I have called you. It is a battle that each of you will face in one way or another. It is one of the greatest battles you will fight."

"Battle," I thought. "I'm not ready for a battle."

Our path continued toward the other two people on the water. Finally, we stood directly in front of a large wall-like mirror that stretched without end across the waves. It was clear that the approaching individuals were reflections of our own images. The mirror also served as a wall that appeared to be impenetrable. I didn't know how we would get past it, but I was sure the Lord had a plan.

Meanwhile, the shouts of joy had grown much louder and the sound of great praise seemed to lie just ahead, beyond the wall-like mirror.

Jesus turned to look at me. "You have to get past this battle over self if you are ever going to walk free in worship."

I looked into the mirror and saw in my reflection everything I knew about myself. All of my imperfections and weaknesses were magnified. I had forgotten all about the waves and storms crashing around us until their reflection in the mirror reminded me of their fury. I knew my focus should not be on the circumstances or on myself, but it all seemed so magnified and tough to handle.

Try as I might, I could not get my focus off myself. I tried looking to the Lord but could not do so without glancing back at the mirror. Guilt and shame mocked me. I started to see how unworthy I was. Just then, a wave of His grace reached up and splashed me in the face. For a moment my perspective was quickened; still, I struggled to win this battle.

I began to recognize that this reflection also revealed my greatest gifts and accomplishments. I tried to concentrate on these things in order to forget my imperfections, but as I did, I began to sink. I remembered how much the Lord dislikes pride and I realized that it was separating me from Him. Confused, depressed, and emptied by discouragement, I stood weak and helpless before this great obstacle—*me*.

I was exhausted and wanted so badly to get past myself. I became weaker and almost unable to stand. Fighting to stand by the grace all around me, I leaned over to my left and rested on the shoulder of the Lord. From this dependent position, I opened my eyes and became aware of much more than just my own reflection.

My eyes confirmed that Jesus was still standing right beside me. He had been all along; He never left my side. In His reflection, the Lord's smile stretched from ear to ear. This alone was enough to keep my eye contact fixed on Him. I lifted my head from His shoulder and walked closer to the mirror. The Lord's reflection grew larger with every step. There was so much to see in His image; I saw so much of what He encompassed. The images in His reflection did not reveal what was just behind us, but shed light on what was just ahead.

I stooped to my knees and began to sob. This mirror was not a mirror at all. It was a window. I couldn't see what was ahead because I had allowed my reflection to obscure the greater vision. The longer I would choose to focus on myself, the more I would miss out on.

Mighty sounds roared on the other side of the window. Heavenly worship consumed everything that stood on these waters of grace. I couldn't wait to join the group that sang unto the Lord.

He lifted me into His arms and pressed me to His heart. "You are about to begin walking in your calling. Remember, only I can place you in the right place. You won't find it on your own."

Once I was in His arms, He walked right through the window as though it didn't exist. The sight I had seen through Him let me know that whatever was ahead was glorious.

Limp in His arms, I fell asleep as we crossed to the other side.

Chapter 10

A TALL TOWER

I DIDN'T KNOW WHAT to do next, so I began to inquire of the Lord. "Father, please teach me Your ways. Please show me how to join You where You are moving. Where do I go from here? Please, help me."

Like a solid rumble in my heart, I heard Him very clearly say, "Step."

So I did. My foot crunched in hard rubble that scattered under it. Except for one beaming light in the center of the debris, dim shadows were cast over all that I could see. As I walked toward the light, I saw the remains of strong and heavy foundations, pieces of walls still trying to stand erect, and a large piece of a tower that lay over much of the rubble. The place wasn't dark, but dim, and the one beaming light stood out strongly and with clear direction. It stretched down from farther away than I could see, perhaps straight from Heaven. Under the light I saw a plaque of iron and bronze that had been crushed into hundreds of pieces; yet every piece remained aligned, still revealing the plaque's message.

I knelt down, released a gentle puff from my mouth to scatter the dust, and found the following engraving:

Come, let us build ourselves a city, with a tower that reaches to the heavens, so that we may make a name for ourselves and not be scattered over the face of the whole earth.

I was awestruck as I recognized the words from Genesis 11:4— the plaque was from the Tower of Babel!

"Hello," a voice said from behind. "You have arrived. I have been waiting for you. This is where your assignment begins."

The voice was strong, yet gentle. The presence of the speaker was very calming. It wasn't the Lord, but it was someone very near and dear to Him. I could tell because He carried the Lord's presence.

"I am Abraham," he said with a deep, resonant voice. "You are family, are you not?"

"Well, yes, I suppose I am. I had never really thought of it that way. You are father Abraham, and according to the Bible we are all your descendants."

"Yes, that's true. But not everyone adheres to the line the Lord has drawn through me. You are here because you have the opportunity to be one of my children (see Rom. 9:8). It is time for your assignment to begin."

Abraham's words raised as many questions as answers. "But why here?" I asked. "Why the Tower of Babel? It was a place of such selfishness and confusion. Now look at it…destruction. Isn't that the opposite of the Lord's assignments?"

"Often the greatest light comes from the greatest darkness. What the enemy intends for evil, our God surely uses for His good.[1] The Tower of Babel is the ultimate symbol of man's pride and reliance upon self. They wanted to build their own way to Heaven, but lost sight of their dependence upon God. They tried to lift themselves up instead of waiting for the Lord to lift them up. It was a terrible tragedy, a great lesson, and an even better strategy. You've read about the tragedy and now you have seen it with your own eyes. Now you must understand the lesson.

"We are in the days of Elijah. The spirit of Elijah prepares the way of the Lord. Just as Elijah prepared and gave way to the Christlike ministry of Elisha, John the Baptist prepared the way of the Lord Jesus Christ.

"Rising up now is the generation that will prepare the way of the young ones—His simple yet wonderful children. They will walk as a generation in greater ministry than Elisha; and as Jesus Himself prophesied, they will do greater works than He did during His earthly walk.[2] The enemy has tried to smite this generation of the Lord's beloved ones, but He has protected them for such a time as this.

"These children are the lambs that roar. The Lion of Judah will give a mighty roar through this childlike army. It is your assignment to join the Lord in preparing the way for these children to walk in their purposes and callings. Many are still held in some form of captivity; but the Lord has put their release in motion, and you are part of this. It comes at a great price, but with the greatest of rewards. This is where the lesson of the Tower of Babel becomes so important.

"None of us is above this lesson, which is part of the reason I am here to share it with you. The lesson must be learned if you are to be part of the great move God is bringing forth with His children.

"You see, when I went to Hagar in hope of having a child,[3] I stopped looking at the Lord, if only for a moment. It was a grave mistake on my part. I couldn't see how God's promise would come about, so I acted in my human wisdom, trying to build what God had promised.[4]

"We must always wait for God to establish His will and His Kingdom. And we must be careful not to go ahead of His timing. *Trust* means that we allow God to stay in control, and we join Him, not the other way around. The question to you is this: Do you want to build yourself a tower, or do you want to join God in building His Kingdom?"

I had forgotten that even faithful Abraham had taken a grievously ill-advised step. It served as a great reminder that I, too, could make faulty human decisions if I took my eyes off the Lord.

"His Kingdom!" I exclaimed. "Of course I want to build His Kingdom."

"That is good. But you missed the most important part of the question. It was not as much about your choice between a tower and His Kingdom, but rather whether you would *build by yourself* or *build with God*.

"Most begin with the intention of building His Kingdom, but they do so in their own strength and wisdom. God has a different set of plans, far different timing, and His ways are certainly above our human ways.[5] You can work to build His Kingdom and still end up building yourself a tower. But when we build with God we will always see His promises brought to life."

Abraham continued, intently focused on the lesson. "Perhaps you have read in the Book of Hebrews, chapter six, verse twelve, where it says: *'imitate those who through faith and patience inherit the promises.*[6] That was my problem. I walked long in faith, but lost the patience for a time. Inheriting God's promises and seeing them brought to life requires both faith and patience."

For fear of saying something else that was wrong, I just nodded. I didn't want to speak or step in error. The last thing I wanted to do was get ahead of God, or build something of self. It was easier to stand back.

"I understand the fear you are now facing," Abraham said, quickly answering my thoughts. "But sitting back in fear will also keep you from seeing His promises brought to life. What good is patience without His faith? The two must work together for anyone to work with Him."

Though I was beginning to understand, I still thought it best, at least for the moment, to keep quiet and listen.

"The lesson you must learn from the Tower of Babel is this: You and your generation have a very special role to play in God's plan. That role, however, is contrary to the tendencies of man. As I said before, these are the days of Elijah, and you are among those who will prepare the way for God's best. There could be no greater calling—yet man's tendency is to want to be the best.

"You and your generation can seek to have a great impact and do great things, but you will only be building a tower. To build with God, you must see His potential rather than your own, and you must build toward what you cannot yet see. This role affords no notoriety. It demands perseverance and will require you to live in daily trust and surrender. But it is the greatest of callings. You will be serving God by serving His upcoming generation, in whom you will see His greatest promises fulfilled. You and that generation need one another."

Abraham continued. The gravity of his words was evident. "Many have attempted to walk in these ways, but have quickly succumbed to the pressures of pride that drove them to build for themselves. Many feel like they must leave something behind that can be seen by men. But eye has not seen, nor ear heard, nor has entered into the hearts of man the things which God has planned for those who love Him.[7]

"The Lord is not about buildings, but movements! If you will take your eyes away from yourself and what you can build, and if you will instead cast your vision toward Him and His ways, you will help prepare the way for many—even those who seem unlikely but are waiting to be released out of captivity and into their callings. Bless them, believe in them, help them, and run with them toward the Lord. Stand by their side as they learn who God has created them to be. Prepare the way of the Lord, believe in His children."

My questions burst forth: "But how do I keep from building a tower? How will I know how to stay on the right path? If you could be taken astray, even for a moment, how much more could I do the same? I want to walk this path and I want to prepare the way, but I don't know where to begin. It almost feels like starting over again. I can't do it alone."

"You have the fear of the Lord; this is a good thing. Just start with Him. Go back to Jesus each day and keep your eyes on Him, your first love. If you do this with every step, you will not move from the path that is His grace. Do not even focus on the vision at hand, but on God alone. He will lead you, but you must abide in Him.

"Whatever you do, do not look at self. Remember how much damage this caused you in your recent experiences with captivity. When you feel discouraged, confused, depressed, or overly burdened—or when any negative feeling challenges your faith—it is an indication that you are looking toward self. Put your eyes immediately back on the Lord and you will be just fine."

Not wanting to leave his presence without all he'd come to give me, I asked, "Abraham?"

"Yes, go on."

"Earlier, when you told me what this place meant...about the Tower of Babel...you said it was a tragedy, a lesson, and a strategy. I'm beginning to understand the first two, but how can this monument to self be strategic?"

"I was just about to get to that, but I wanted to make sure you understood its lesson first. The plaque you were drawn to says far more than words about self uttered by builders of a tower to the heavens. As much as it is a lesson from the past, it is also a picture into the future.

"Remember, God works all things together for good, to those who love Him.[8] What the enemy meant here for evil, God destroyed, with a plan to use it for good.[9]

"Did you see how the plaque was shattered into hundreds of pieces? Did you wonder how each piece was brought back together to form one image? Each piece, as you can imagine, had been scattered through the rubble. But God brought it back together so that people like you could learn His lessons from it. It is the very same with those whom He scattered with confusion across the face of the earth.

"They had come together to be one people under one language. Their oneness gave them tremendous power and authority. But their vision was misdirected toward self, which bred evil in their hearts. They had to be scattered across the nations. Yet God never lost sight of where one of those people went. His priority is the whole world. Scattering the people planted seeds so that when the time was right, His generation of children would rise up all across the nations. God's vision is for the whole of the world—*all* His people. Your vision must become the same.

"Just as you have seen each broken piece of the plaque brought back together to form a message under His beaming light, you will also see His broken people, His children, brought back together from all over the earth to represent His image to the world. From Him, they will be a light unto the nations. God never breaks down something or someone without the hope to see them rebuilt. One of the greatest tragedies this world has ever known will soon be brought back together by the Lord to reveal a tremendous strategy. The pieces may seem scattered now, but they will soon be released from their brokenness to come together as a vessel of His light.

"He has prepared the way. Now you must join Him and do the same."

Chapter 11

FREEDOM?

"LORD, HOW COULD I end up back here in this prison! One moment I feel like I am flourishing with You, and in the next breath, I wake up in my self-made prison cell. Lord, I vowed that I would never come back to this place."

I sat in prison again, surrounded with its huge bars and wretched walls. My chains felt more painful than ever. Maybe it was because I now knew they were there. The shrieking of other captives hurt not only my ears, but also my heart. Their pain was one thing; their obvious lack of hope and dreams was another. To my ears it sounded like uproarious yelling, but to my heart it was the cry of Esau pleading, "Bless me too, Father" (see Gen. 27:36).

Why was I back here? My frustration possessed me. Then my thoughts halted as the Lord's Word hidden in my heart popped up before it: *"Be still, and know that I am God"* (Ps. 46:10).

I recited the Scripture over and over again to reel in its truth at that moment. I knew it was the Spirit's prompting. I gathered myself from the uprising I felt inside and knelt down to the floor.

"Please give me Your wisdom, Jesus. Please show me Your way. Help me to see more of You, Lord, and less of myself. Forgive me, Jesus. Take my will."

Suddenly, I remembered: It is *my* choice. I can leave my captivity at any time, but I have to believe. Beyond believing, I needed to walk in that belief. As the Lord had so encouraged me, I had to walk by faith and not by sight,[1] knowing that He would go with me and help me.

Just as my faith actively rose up, a light shone at my feet. In the light was a simple, tattered, tied-up scroll. I took the light as a sign from the Lord, believing that this scroll was something from Him. If I was back in this prison yet again, there had to be a purpose. Perhaps the scroll contained a special key or instruction.

Slowly, but excitedly, I reached down to pick up the scroll. It was very light in weight and I could already see inscriptions and pictures inside. I began unraveling it gently, careful not to tear the delicate paper. With the scroll fully extended, I tilted it toward the light shining into my cell.

It was a map! But it was not just any map. It was a map of the prison. It had a picture of my cell, the hallway, the Mess Hall, the outside yard, and the door that had been marked "Freedom?" There was even a picture of the life and world just outside of the prison door. But the pictures weren't mere images. Each one bore an inscription.

Across the picture of my cell and other cells was written: "Loose the bonds of injustice."[2] Written all down the hallway it read: "Take away the yoke from your midst; the pointing of the finger, and speaking wickedness."[3] Through the thick walls of the cells the command read: "Undo the heavy burdens."[4]

The slop buffet in the Mess Hall was circled on the map. An arrow pointed to it and the words: "Share your bread with the hungry."[5] And written over all the tables where inmates griped and complained, it said: "Extend your soul to the hungry and satisfy the afflicted soul."[6]

In The Yard area of the map I was reminded: "Let the oppressed go free!"[7] Written along the perimeters was the statement: "When you see the naked, cover him, and do not hide yourself from your own flesh."[8]

At the door marked "Freedom?" I was strengthened and encouraged by the words: "Then you shall call, and the LORD will answer; you shall cry, and He will say, 'Here I am.'"[9] And just outside that door and that promise, on the other side of the prison, the map was inscribed again: "Those from among you shall build the old waste places; you shall raise up the foundations of many generations; and you shall be called the Repairer of the Breach, the Restorer of Streets to Dwell In."[10]

Like beams of light, the truths of this map shot through my heart and mind. I understood the map. I could see the need and the journey that was before me. Not only would this map set me free from this place, but my freedom would free others. The Lord and others had taught me; but now I could see it all right before my eyes.

I stood up with a new confidence, looked at the bars before me, and left the hopeless walls behind. The bars parted like the Red Sea and the guard could only stop me if I let him. My chains were gone. The Lord had washed them away and nothing could hinder me as long as I walked by faith. I remembered that it was not enough to be forgiven; I had to live forgiven. That was the entire premise of the Red Sea. If I did not walk by faith upon the sea of grace, then I would never truly walk.

I walked away from the burdensome walls of my past; they could shame me no longer. My chains were left piled in the corner.

The bars of unbelief could no longer contain me, but were now behind me. I followed the map specifically, and wanted to go to each spot that was marked.

As I walked down the hallway from my cell, I saw once again the man I had known previously, the one I had helped to bind with my criticism and judgment. I stopped before him and looked directly at him, expecting a response. But he did not recognize me. It did not matter.

"I am sorry!" I pleaded. "You may not remember me, but I remember you from many years ago. These chains, they are not yours. I and others gave them to you, but we were wrong. You have been created for so much more, and God has already loosened your chains. Forgive me for keeping them on you. Would you mind if I prayed over you?"

He cautiously affirmed my request. I laid my hand upon him and began to pray. After we finished praying, his face lit up. He was like a lighthouse that had been dark for many years. He let go of his chains immediately; I watched them fall to his side. He smiled at me with a nod, but didn't say a thing. He walked forward in a new way. I watched in joy as he left his chains behind.

I went straight for the Mess Hall. I walked over to the line and looked again at the lies and garbage they were feeding people. I couldn't feed them the lies that were so conveniently available; I had to feed the captives with the bread God had given me. When I looked again at what was written across the tables on the map, it made sense to me: "Extend your soul to the hungry and satisfy the afflicted soul."[11] I had to give them what Jesus had given me.

All this time, through this whole journey, the Lord had been feeding the Bread of Life—the Bread that satisfies—to my soul. The prisoners here complained so much only because nothing they ate ever satisfied them. But if I simply extended what was already inside of me, their hunger would be satisfied.

"There's more!" I blurted out to the captives at a table. "Look up from yourself and see the plan and purpose God has for your life."

I spoke to the next table: "Taste and see that the LORD is good.[12] He has released us not only to salvation, but to lives of purpose and promise! Run with Jesus! Join Him now! He wants to fill you, and He has called you to help fill others."

I extended my hands away from where they grasped my heart, as if presenting Him to the prisoners. Little did I know that as I poured out my heart, God presented them with food. Just as my hands motioned toward them, a fresh loaf of bread appeared on each plate, a full glass of juice appeared beside it, and a fish, prepared and ready to eat, graced each place setting. It was a miracle! I spoke and gave out of my soul, and the Lord provided a sign and answered every doubt. The prisoners who were eating jumped up—a plate in one hand and a glass in the other. They ate joyfully of the Lord's gift and streamed out the Mess Hall doors, wanting more of what God had ahead.

The map came alive. I could hardly believe my eyes. The Spirit of God brought His truths to life!

The next spot on the map was The Yard. I walked out the doorway to the heavily gated area and felt my heart ask the Lord for guidance. At His prompting, I looked over to the outer perimeter where a man was lying in the rain gutter. He was burning up and without clothes to protect him from the heat. I walked over, glanced back at the map, looked again to the man, and saw the naked whom I was commanded to cover. I didn't have extra clothes, but I couldn't hide myself from my own flesh. I took off my shirt and bent down next to him.

"Jesus loves you." I said simply. "His blood covers your pain. Be oppressed no more. You are free! Jesus has called you by name. Rise and shine. That is what He has created you for."

I walked away slowly, looking back at the man as I did. He jumped for joy from where he was lying. Up and down in the air he fluttered like jumping jacks, reflecting the light of God. Everyone in The Yard froze and watched, witnessing full and true freedom for the very first time. The man ran to the center of The Yard, where all the other prisoners gathered around him.

The man began to shout words no one would have suspected he knew: "Where the Spirit of the Lord is, *there is freedom!*"[13] The other prisoners could not help but jump for joy with him. The transformation of God was happening among us.

No matter how much I wanted to stop and watch the scene, I had to follow the map the Lord had sent. I walked straight toward the door marked "Freedom?" It was closer than it had been my last time here. The warden spoke, but I ignored the words with which he attempted to burden me. I knew they were lies. I continued toward the door and reached for it.

Suddenly, a light went off in my heart and I stopped. I realized that I didn't need to walk out the door marked "Freedom?" in order to be free. I was set free the moment I chose to believe in and trust Him more than I trusted myself or what the world had taught me. It was clear that with real trust and faith, I was free to live in a whole different world. It was then that a deeper truth finally hit me: As I paused to look around, I realized this place wasn't a prison at all. It was the world that we live in, a world filled with His children, believers and unbelievers alike who needed to be loved, valued, and believed in.

The world was revealed for what it had become: our prison, a place that lured us into its patterns of compromise, conformity, and lies. But the world was also the place where our marching orders would cause Jesus's light and glory to be seen. The Warden was using us against each other to keep us from seeing who we are in Christ. The prison was all a lie. He is the truth, and He empowered me by His Spirit to walk in His steps.

Just as the map instructed, I stood at the door previously marked "Freedom?" but saw that the question mark had been removed. Freedom was all around us. We were the ones who had created our captivity and kept ourselves hidden from God's best. The map's instructions were clear: "Then you shall call, and the LORD will answer; you shall cry, and He will say, 'Here I am.'"[14]

I stood at the door and looked up. I opened my mouth and let out a great shout to God. It was a shout like none I had ever cried before: *"I'mmmmmm readyeeeeeeeeee!"* I shouted. I was ready to join Him in His best for my life. It was a freedom cry. And just as I finished the drawn-out bellow from the deepest part of me, the Lord answered, saying, "Here I am."

"You cannot serve both God and man,"[15] I heard spoken aloud. "Do you trust Me enough to stop walking in the ways of the world? Do you trust in Me now more than you trust in what your eyesight shows you? My ways are higher than your ways and My thoughts are above your thoughts.[16] Put faith before sight and you will be called crazy. Wait for Me to move when the world says you are lagging behind, and you will be judged for your laziness and lack of success. On the other hand, make decisions based on comfort or happiness, and you will not necessarily be on the right path.

"Listen to Me for the fresh and the new each day, and you will truly live. Do not remember the former things, nor consider the things of old. Behold, I will do a new thing, now it shall spring forth, shall you not know it? I will even make a road in the wilderness and rivers in the desert.[17] Look to find Me in the box, the cell you have kept yourself in, and I will be with you—but you will not be with Me until you reach out with a trust that stretches beyond yourself.

"In the days ahead, you who choose the narrow path[18] will find that its limited width is only one of its obstacles. You will also be walking against the grain. With even more effort than treading water against a mighty current, you will be called to follow Me closely as you hear My voice. You will feel and see believers and unbelievers rushing and bumping past you upon the path of the earth, motioning at you as though you were a car riding on the wrong side of the road.

"Upon My path you must not form opinions about anyone. Rather you must know that they were created in My image with a passion, a purpose, and many treasures inside. When you judge even one of these, you judge Me. If you hear about them or discern something that is out of My will, lift them to Me and intercede before you intervene. To form your own opinion becomes judgment. You must take your focus off what people are or are not doing and bless them for who they are. What someone *does* is of the world's influence; but who they *are* is of My creation. And greater am I who is in you than he who is in the world.[19] You must help the *who* overtake the *what*.

"This generation—you included—will be part of a revolution that must be fought with love. Again, My child, after these many journeys we have taken and experiences you have had, I say again to you that you are to bless. You stand here with Me among captives who have underestimated the simple secret of their release. Go out and bless the captives with freedom, with truth, with love, and with light so they might know that I have released them. And remember, I love you!"

We stepped through the frame where the door once hung. When I saw what was there, a flood of God's Spirit caused every part of me to tingle. All those from inside, the ones who were captive and enslaving one another, were now out here. They were like an army of God who had been raised up for such a time as this. They were in the harvest fields rebuilding old waste places. They were raising once again the foundations of many generations dismissed by the world, even the foundations of the early Church of Acts. They were repairing all that was broken and working together toward redemption of what had been lost. They were restoring the streets from darkness to light!

I had never seen such a scene. But I sensed God in it. I could no longer see Him next to me, but I saw Him all around. He was in each person, each captive who had been released. He was using each one to release others. These were the sons and daughters of the living God!

And I was one of them.

In a cold sweat, I woke up in my room, slightly overwhelmed but very inspired. How long had I lived a lie? Where should I start? What could I do? The obvious struck me when I glanced at the floor. The only place to start was on my face before the Lord. The waiting and listening started now. I rolled from my comfortable position sprawled across my bed and went to my face on the floor.

I paused silently for several minutes, seeking to draw nearer to Him, and said, "Jehovah God, please show me how I can join You today."

EPILOGUE

JESUS IS THE ULTIMATE model for releasing the captives. His testimony shows us the steps we must walk in and the love that must be lived out beyond our words. Revelation 19:10 says, *"The testimony of Jesus is the spirit of prophecy."*

First, Jesus lived His life releasing the captives, including you and me. He gave us freedom, and in doing so, He gave us everything we need to join Him in releasing others. He has given each of us a testimony of Christ's redemption in our lives. This is the testimony we must use to multiply and release others in the name of Jesus, and by the power and leading of the Holy Spirit. Jesus's testimony becomes prophetic through our lives.

How has the Lord released you? What is your testimony? From what bondages or lies has He delivered you? How has His love washed over you? How has He filled you up, and how is He using you to multiply His love to others? Whatever the testimony of Jesus in your life, you have the authority, calling, and commissioning to release it to others. Jesus's testimony in your life prophesies what is possible for others who are caught in the same battles and captivity you have experienced.

Did God meet you through acts of love? Did He use someone to bring you healing or deliverance? Did God provide for you in a seemingly impossible situation? Was it through the outreach of a group Bible study or local church? What are the fingerprints of God on your life and your release to freedom? How does He want to multiply it to others?

There are so many different ways in which each of us has been held captive. Likewise, there are so many ways in which each of us has been released. We display the testimony of Jesus in our lives, because our freedom points to our having been released by Him. Now we must release that testimony to others and join Him in releasing the captives!

Look at the testimony in Moses's life of what God used, not only to release him, but also to take him from being a captive to being more than a conqueror (see Rom. 8:37). Moses was an imperfect vessel, and he knew it. His faith was imperfect too, but that was what God was trying to change. Even when the Lord came and met with Moses at the burning bush (see Exod. 3), Moses clung to his fear-based captivity. He doubted his usefulness to God because of insecurity, because of his past, because of the lies he believed about himself, and because of his own unbelief. Moses was called by God Himself to release the captives, but he could not fulfill this commissioning until he himself took his own fears and insecurities captive and watched God transform them to His glory.

In Exodus 4:1, Moses asked the Lord, *"But suppose they will not believe me or listen to my voice; suppose they say, 'The LORD has not appeared to you'"* (NKJV). Can you remember a time when God spoke to you about moving forward, and you said the same thing

Moses did? Our answers might sound slightly different, but the motivation is the same: "But suppose this...or that..." Or "what if...?" Fear keeps us focused on the world's ways of thinking, while God is ready for us to believe Him and move forward, just as He called Moses to do.

> So the LORD said to him, "What is that in your hand?" He said, "A rod." And He said, "Cast it on the ground." So he cast it on the ground, and it became a serpent; and Moses fled from it. Then the LORD said to Moses, "Reach out your hand and take it by the tail" (and he reached out his hand and caught it, and it became a rod in his hand), "that they may believe that the LORD God of their fathers, the God of Abraham, the God of Isaac, and the God of Jacob, has appeared to you" (Exodus 4:2-5 NKJV).

I find it so very interesting and challenging that God did a miracle with the rod to increase Moses's faith, and also turned the rod into, of all things, a serpent. The serpent, of course, has represented the devil and his lies since the beginning of time. The rod-turned-serpent was not an attack of the enemy, as there never was any real threat to Moses. It was, however, a test from God able to turn the gaps of fear in Moses's life into a more seamless, whole faith.

This was Moses's everyday rod, a tool he had used often and knew well. But when God first turned it into a serpent, Moses fled from it. Look at this! God was in the middle of doing something and Moses almost let his fear drive him away from what God was doing. He almost missed out on God's timing and opportunity.

And yet, there's more. God did not turn the rod back to its original state while it was on the ground. The Lord told Moses to reach out his hand and take the serpent by the tail. Moses had to overcome his fear in order to see God transform the supposed threat into a rod of authority in his hand. Only after Moses had taken hold of his own fears could he release others through faith.

Moses had used the rod many times, but it was a different rod now. Even more importantly, he was a different Moses! Just as his rod was transformed from a natural instrument to a supernatural one, Moses went from being a natural, insecure person to being a vessel of supernatural authority. He conquered his fear and moved immediately from the position of captive into his calling as leader. By walking with God in this way, Moses would release a whole generation of captives from their bondage.

Once the fears in Moses's life were transformed into faith, anything was possible! He now understood how fear could be overcome. He had a testimony that gave him the faith to release others; it was a supernatural tool God used to multiply faith in a whole generation of Israelites.

Now it is our turn to pick up the testimony of Jesus, take fear by the tail, lift up the rod God has given us, and release the captives with whom we interact, walk, and live on a daily basis. Many of us don't know where to start: It is where Jesus began—with those around Him.

Jesus went to the down and out, those in bondage to the world and its lies. There were outward bondages, such as sickness, poverty, and sin, and still deeper and sometimes hidden bondages of fear, doubt, shame, guilt, condemnation, and oppression.

Jesus began with His disciples and then went to the "least of these" (see Matt. 25:40). Wherever He went, He lived out acts of love, healing, and deliverance; these were the ways in which He released the captives from what bound them. This in turn increased belief among the multitudes. The faith of one captive was able to free that person and often multiplied to release many more who watched love come to life. Jesus started with those who were open and those who were in need. He poured His love into whomever God placed in front of Him.

With regard to releasing the captives, the Lord has imparted to us three basic principles that we are called to impart to others as we walk with Him—where He walked and the way that He walked. (The Appendix will expand upon these principles and provide practical suggestions to help you bring these principles to life in *your* walk with Christ.)

1. See people through God's perspective—Look for the light that is burning inside someone and trying to get out. Do not look at the external circumstances, limits, or impossibilities. Instead, look at the light of God that is shining deep within. Have you ever sat in a dark room and placed a flashlight under a fully closed fist? Your hand swallows the light in its darkness, yet you can see the light burning inside and earnestly trying to escape through any and every available crack or crevice. I believe this is similar to how God sees opportunities in us. He sees the light, the treasures He placed in us when He created us in His image. The clasping strength or smothering darkness of the flesh is no deterrent to His light. It is too powerful to be contained. The Lord is drawn to bring that light out of each of us. We must see others with those same eyes.

2. Listen—Listen to the Holy Spirit's promptings and direction in your heart. Listen to the story, the pain, and the need of the person. One of my life Scriptures is found in John 5:19: *"Jesus answered and said to them, 'Most assuredly, I say to you, the Son can do nothing of Himself, but what He sees the Father do; for whatever He does, the Son also does in like manner'"* (NKJV). Jesus walked every day of His life in obedient oneness with the Father, never presuming His own ways but aligning with the path where God was moving. Jesus always joined the Father where He was moving and He did this through incredible closeness. I want to do the same. If I am going to join God where He is moving I must know how to listen to God's voice and the promptings of the Holy Spirit in my heart. He will show me the way. He will tell me where. He will show me whom. He will tell me how. If I know how to listen to God according to His Word, is there anything else I need?

But I must also listen to the people God directs me to. I cannot be about my own agenda. I have to be about God's agenda. Sometimes I can't listen to God unless I first listen to others. When we listen to the person to whom God directs us, we give them love, we give them value, and we may find a hurt that God wants to heal. Just listen! Obey Him. Then trust Him with the results.

3. Love them! Love them! Love them! We want to minister to people, but that's not always what they need. Most people don't need to be ministered to; they need to be loved. There is a big difference! When we minister, true and effective love does not always occur. But when we love someone, the best kind of ministry always happens. Love never fails (see 1 Cor. 13:8).

There are many ways to join the Lord and release the captives. If we will draw close to God and ask Him, He will show us how, where, and when. You may already have a simple rod or testimony in your hand that God wants to multiply to many others. The following Appendix, entitled "Pray:58," is an action-step model of how we can begin to walk as Jesus walked, and where He walked. It models just one way to love as He has loved—and one way to release the captives by living out the Word of God in their midst, just as Jesus did. His testimony comes to life in and through us by the power of His living Word and His Holy Spirit. He's waiting for you.

> *The Spirit of the* LORD *God is upon Me, because the* LORD *has anointed Me to preach good tidings to the poor; He has sent Me to heal the brokenhearted, to proclaim liberty to the captives, and the opening of the prison to those who are bound; to proclaim the acceptable year of the* LORD (Isaiah 61:1-2 NKJV).

Appendix

PRAY:58
LIVE ACTION STEPS FOR RELEASING THE CAPTIVES

Is this not the fast that I have chosen: To loose the bonds of wickedness, to undo the heavy burdens, to let the oppressed go free, and that you break every yoke? Is it not to share your bread with the hungry, and that you bring to your house the poor who are cast out; when you see the naked, that you cover him, and not hide yourself from your own flesh? Then your light shall break forth like the morning, your healing shall spring forth speedily, and your righteousness shall go before you; the glory of the LORD shall be your rear guard. Then you shall call, and the LORD will answer; you shall cry, and He will say, "Here I am." If you take away the yoke from your midst, the pointing of the finger, and speaking wickedness, if you extend your soul to the hungry and satisfy the afflicted soul, then your light shall dawn in

*the darkness, and your darkness shall be as the noonday.
The* LORD *will guide you continually, and satisfy your
soul in drought, and strengthen your bones; you shall be
like a watered garden, and like a spring of water, whose
waters do not fail. Those from among you shall build
the old waste places; you shall raise up the foundations of
many generations; and you shall be called the Repairer
of the Breach, the Restorer of Streets to Dwell In. If you
turn away your foot from the Sabbath, from doing your
pleasure on My holy day, and call the Sabbath a delight,
the holy day of the* LORD *honorable, and shall honor
Him, not doing your own ways, nor finding your own
pleasure, nor speaking your own words, then you shall
delight yourself in the* LORD; *and I will cause you to
ride on the high hills of the earth, and feed you with the
heritage of Jacob your father. The mouth of the* LORD
has spoken" (Isaiah 58:6-14 NKJV).

INTRODUCTION

When our family first made our home in Addis Ababa, Ethiopia, it was very important to us not to come and start a ministry or a program, but to come and ask the Lord where He was moving and how we could join Him in His steps.

As we inquired of the Lord, He took us back to Isaiah 58:6-14. We felt as if God was calling us to an unusual sort of fast. To begin our calling in Ethiopia, we would fast for 40 days from all organized ministry and programs. Our only ministry during this time would be to fast from self and try to walk and live out the fast of love described in the verses in Isaiah 58.

When we saw the streets of Addis Ababa, we were reminded of many of the descriptions of the streets where Jesus walked during His time here on earth. We also saw that the map or path through Isaiah 58 looked a lot like the path Jesus walked every day. This would be our fast: to walk the streets of Addis Ababa for 40 days in prayer and abiding fellowship with God, hoping to live out His love toward the people all around us.

As we walked, we asked God to show us His people from His perspective. We asked God to teach us His love for each one. We asked God to teach us to hear His voice and to show us how to live out the promises of His Word in the streets. We asked Jesus to teach us how to join Him in the streets and marketplaces around us, which appeared so much like the streets and marketplaces that He lived in. Very simply, we wanted to walk with Jesus and love like Jesus across the "map" of Isaiah 58.

A CHALLENGE OF LOVE

But go and learn what this means: "I desire mercy and not sacrifice." For I did not come to call the righteous, but sinners, to repentance (Matthew 9:13 NKJV).

What an incredible challenge put forth by Jesus, one that we believe He asks of us even now: *"Go and learn what this means: 'I desire mercy and not sacrifice.'"* Many times we have gone to the Lord through prayer and His Word to learn what this means. Every time, we seem to come up with the same answer: Jesus wants love, not religion—love!

This verse is a perfect parallel to the fast God calls us to in Isaiah 58:6-14. The whole passage speaks to acts of mercy and love, and these acts are the fast He has chosen. This is the fast that He lived. Too often, fasting has become a religious exercise for us. We fast in order to gain, or to meet a religious requirement. But this fast God calls us to in Isaiah 58 is a fast of love, a fast from self. The Gospel that Jesus walked through looks very similar to the map we can follow in Isaiah 58. If we want to walk with Christ and live as He lived, this may be a map of love we can follow.

A big question then becomes, "How?" How do we walk this path of love and mercy that God is calling us to live? I believe the disciples asked this very question of "how" as Jesus prepared to depart from them. This is how Jesus answered them, and how I believe He answers us today:

> *It is to your advantage that I go away; for if I do not go away, the Helper will not come to you; but if I depart, I will send Him to you. And when He has come, He will convict the world of sin, and of righteousness, and of judgment.... I still have many things to say to you, but you cannot bear them now. However, when He, the Spirit of truth, has come, He will guide you into all truth; for He will not speak on His own authority, but whatever He hears He will speak; and He will tell you things to come. He will glorify Me, for He will take of what is Mine and declare it to you* (John 16:7-8;12-14 NKJV).

Jesus is, of course, speaking of His Holy Spirit. Many of us think it would be easier to live like Jesus if we could see Him right here by our side. But Jesus Himself tells us that it is to our advantage that He went away, because He sent us the Helper. He will take that which is of Jesus and declare it to us. He will help us to live out the life Christ called us to follow Him in living.

If we will learn to love like Jesus, with Jesus, we must learn to be disciples of His Holy Spirit. We must live the abiding prayer relationship of which Jesus speaks in John 15, one chapter before His promise of the Holy Spirit. He says that if we will abide in Him, we will bear much fruit and that it will be fruit that remains. (See John 15:5,16.) If we want to walk the streets and marketplaces with Jesus the way He walked them, we must learn a deep and interactive prayer relationship with God so He can show us His way.

The more time we take to be still with God in prayer, the more we will learn to know His voice. We will learn His love and His perspective. We will begin to further understand His ways and His truth. He will teach us how to pray, and His Spirit and His Presence will refine us to be more like Him. But this only happens when we take time to get to know Him better in prayer and the Word. If we truly want to learn *how* to walk this path, we must spend more time alone with God. If we will learn to abide in Christ, He will show us how to walk His path that yields the fruit of love, a love that never fails.

Daniel 11:32 reads: *"The people who know their God shall be strong, and carry out great exploits"* (NKJV). What a simple but powerful equation. If we become people who *know* God intimately through our lives, our decisions, our steps, and our love, we will carry out great exploits for the benefit of the world around us. If we want to walk like Jesus, and with Jesus, we must know Jesus more closely.

This Appendix can serve as a guide to help you continue to learn how to love *like Jesus* and *with Jesus* across the map of Isaiah 58. We have pulled out for you (and we are living ourselves) 12 steps from Isaiah 58:6-14. Each step is broken down to give you examples, testimonies, descriptions, guidance in prayer, and practical application. The goal of this Appendix is not just to learn the concepts found in Isaiah 58. The ultimate goal is to live the Word by sharing with the world around us the love this passage describes—and to do it on an everyday basis.

The streets around you may be filled with people and circumstances that resemble those described in the Gospels. This is certainly true in Addis Ababa. Not everyone lives in a place with streets and marketplaces that look like those through which Jesus walked. However, all of us live near people who are in some sort of need; you might need to take a few extra steps to get there. These steps might not be easy or convenient, but they will be worth it. Jesus's world is all around us. Sometimes we have to learn to take a step back and see people and circumstances through His eyes instead of our own.

Please use wisdom and discernment in your choices as you follow these steps. Ask God to guide you and protect you each step of the way. As is recommended throughout the Appendix, please go through the steps with at least one prayer partner alongside you. There are tremendous possibilities when we enter into prayer together—God's love and His power are multiplied!

Most of all, as you walk out this map of Isaiah 58 with the Lord, allow Him to stretch your love. Remember, this is a fast from self. It may be very challenging at first, but these are the steps that Jesus has walked. They are steps of faith and they are steps of love. When you feel challenged by the process, remember the promises God gives in the passage. The steps are difficult, but His promises in Isaiah 58:6-14 are incomparable—and we are meant to receive them.

Here is a summary of God's promises as presented in Isaiah 58:6-14 (NKJV):

Our healing shall spring forth speedily (verse 8*).*

Our righteousness shall go before us (verse 8).

The glory of the Lord will be our rear guard (verse 8).

The Lord will answer and say, "Here I am" (verse 9).

Our light will dawn in the darkness (verse 10).

Our darkness shall be as the noonday (verse 10).

The Lord will guide us continually (verse 11).

He will satisfy our souls even in drought (verse 11).

He will strengthen our bones (verse 11).

He will make us like watered gardens (verse 11).

We will be like springs of water whose waters do not fail (verse 11).

Those among us shall build the old waste places (verse 12).

We shall raise up the foundations of many generations (verse 12).

We shall be called Repairers of the Breach and will be Restorers of the Streets to Dwell In (verse 12).

We will ride on the high hills of the earth (verse 14).

God will feed us with the heritage of Jacob our father (verse 14).

REVIVE MY LOVE!

We do not take this journey for the sake of these promises. The only way we can truly take these powerful steps of faith is if our motives are love and mercy. But God will be with us and move through us according to these promises if we will join Him on this path—the pathway of releasing the captives!

Whenever I think of the life of love that Jesus lived or the path of love to which He calls us in Isaiah 58, I cannot help but think of Jesus's discussion with Peter in John 21. Earlier in the chapter, Peter had been part of an incredible miracle. He had been obedient, acted in faith, and had left everything behind to follow Jesus. Yet at this point, Jesus chose to restore Peter's love. The conversation below appears in John 21:15-17 (NKJV):

Jesus asks Peter, *"Do you love Me more than these?"*
Peter then responds, *"Yes, Lord; You know that I love You."*
Jesus answers, *"Feed My lambs."*
Then Jesus asks Peter again, *"Do you love Me?"*
And Peter again responds, *"Yes, Lord; You know that I love You."*
"Tend My sheep," Jesus said.
Then Jesus asked Peter the same question a third time, *"Do you love Me?"*
Peter was now grieved by being asked this again. *"Lord, You know all things; You know that I love You."*
Jesus said to him, *"Feed My sheep."*

I do not necessarily believe that Jesus was questioning Peter's love; I do, however, believe Jesus was challenging Peter's love to rise higher. No matter how much love Peter had shown, no matter what Peter was already doing, Jesus challenged Peter to dig deeper in his faith. Jesus revived Peter's love! Shortly thereafter, Peter followed the steps Jesus had laid out for the disciples and reaped the harvest revealed in the Book of Acts.

When I look at this challenge to Peter I see my own need. Revive my love, Lord! Help my love to rise higher. Help me to dig deeper. Revive my love, Jesus, so that I can join You on the path You have set ahead of me. Revive my love!

If we truly want to see our cities, nations, and even our world changed, we must start walking where Jesus walked; and we must walk with Jesus and like Him. This is the fast that He has chosen; if I am going to partake of this chosen fast, I need God to revive my love.

In the following pages are 12 prayerful and practical steps designed to help you live God's Word in the world around you and release the captives as Jesus did.

STEP 1

Loose the chains of injustice (Isaiah 58:6).

EXPLANATION

The above Scripture quote is from the New International Version. The New King James Version quoted at the outset of the Appendix reads: *"To loose the bonds of wickedness."* Either way, every one of us in every part of the world is surrounded in one way or another by people who are in need, specifically—in need of what only God can do. Many people are in bondage to poverty, sickness, drugs, alcohol, and much more. We are called to be examples, light, and vessels through whom God delivers His love.

"To loose the chains of injustice," means that God has called each of us to help others in their various struggles. And the Bible is a testimony that shows us that injustice is overcome by grace! The world can be very cruel and unjust to many people around us. But with the Lord, we have the opportunity to loosen that injustice.

God has called us to be an extension of His love, grace, and mercy, as these overcome bondage and injustice. Right now there is near each of us someone who is tied down by the things of the world. May God teach us how to join Him in untying them.

PRAYER

Lord, please lead me. I want to walk in Your steps, Jesus, and to live and love as You do, Jesus. Holy Spirit, please teach me and help me to live out this verse from the Bible. May I be a vessel of Your love, grace, and mercy to those who are bound by the chains of the world. Would You please teach me, Lord, how to pray for them? Increase my faith and help me to love them with Your love, Jesus. Thank You, Lord. It is in Jesus's name we pray. Amen.

TESTIMONY

One of our main prayer partners through these steps has been Alex. From the age of 7, Alex grew up on the streets of Addis Ababa. He is now 25 and is a very big part of our family and of the testimony of love that God is raising up. Not long ago, Alex and I were on one of our many walks together through the streets of Addis Ababa. It was toward the end of rainy season, and we had a practical agenda to accomplish as we went. However, we also had a spiritual agenda that was consistent with our many other walks: Walk *with* Jesus and love *like* Jesus. Even though we were doing other things, we had to stay connected to God through prayer so that we would know how to live out Jesus's love in Isaiah 58 that day.

The rain fell in a consistent drizzle as we walked, so our pace was hurried. However, just before we approached a turn we'd planned to take, God directed my gaze to one specific woman sitting on the road. Here in Addis, there are many people living in difficult situations on the streets; however, on that day I felt this was who God wanted us to stop for.

We went over to the woman, knelt down on the curb and introduced ourselves. We asked her name and then asked about her life and how she got there. We asked what her needs were, what pain she was in, and what help she needed from God. She explained that she had come from down country with her husband to find work, but they were unsuccessful. Instead, she sat on the streets in hope of finding provision.

Once we knew her a little better, we asked if she would allow us to pray over her. She gave us permission and we scooted nearer and laid our hands on her. Then Alex translated as I prayed. Many people stopped; some stared. Others gathered around to see what was going on; a few people came close enough to listen. They wondered why we were gathered around her and what had happened to her. We simply prayed the Lord's love and provision over her and we asked God to help her put her full trust in Him. We finished our time together, said our good-byes, and walked away praying for her further. We have no idea what God did in her life, but we do know that she was loved, she was entrusted to God, and the Bible says that this will always yield fruit, even if we can't see it right away.

APPLICATION

(Please note that most of the 12 applications in the coming pages will address ministry to an individual who, for the sake of ease and readability, will be described as "he" or "she." You may be called to minister to someone of either sex in any step.)

Find one person with whom you can pray through and complete the following steps:

- Go out into the public areas near you where you know there are people in need. This might be the streets, the marketplace, around a café, or another area of town.

- Ask God to show you whom He wants to minister to during this time.

- Approach the person He shows you. Introduce yourself and find out what his name is.

- Ask him what is going on in his life.

- Ask what his greatest need is.

- Ask how you can pray for him.

- Ask whether he would allow you to pray over him.

- Gently and carefully lay your hands on him and begin to pray. Hold him up to God and trust Him together.

- Thank the person for sharing his life and time; thank him also for trusting God with you.

- Tell him you will continue to pray for him.

BEFORE YOU GO

Wait on the Lord

Before we can be effective vessels of the Lord, we must take time to be filled with the Lord and His Spirit. Take this time to be alone with God. Ask for His help and ask Him to fill you with His Holy Spirit. Draw close to God and let Him strengthen your love and your faith. Spend at least 20 minutes just to be close to God. The more we know God, the more He will be able to use us as vessels to loosen and break the chains of wickedness for others. Please take this time with God. It's the most important part!

STEP 2

Undo the heavy burdens (Isaiah 58:6 NKJV).

EXPLANATION

Have you ever had a heavy heart? Have you ever felt the weight of difficulty from your circumstances that tries to depress you?

Everyone faces this from time to time, so what are we doing to combat it? Jesus says that His yoke is easy and His burden is light (see Matt. 11:30). If this is true, then we must simply replace the heavy burdens others carry with the light one that Jesus promises. Life doesn't always get easier in that moment, but there is a positive change: The weight of the burden now rests on Jesus's shoulders rather than on the shoulders of a human being.

Isaiah 61:3 talks about giving others the *"garment of praise for the spirit of heaviness"* (NKJV). One of the best ways to help someone get rid of the heavy burdens the world brings is to help them to praise God even when things are hard. Help them find something they are thankful for! Why? Because praising God shows Him that we trust Him and helps people take their eyes off of their heavy burdens. Instead, they can put their eyes on Christ, the One who stands ready to lift those burdens from their shoulders.

We are called by God to *"undo the heavy burdens"* of those around us. The hard part is finished: Jesus accomplished it all! But He waits for us to join Him by faith and help others to lift their burdens up to Him, the One who is ready to carry them.

PRAYER

Lord, please help me to see with Your eyes. Please help me to walk in Your truth. Holy Spirit, lead me to those to whom You want to minister. Lord, there is someone carrying a burden that You want to take away. Please help me to join You by faith in his or her life. Please teach me how to pray, and how to live with a thankful heart and spirit toward You. Help me to join You in undoing someone's heavy burdens. In Jesus's name I pray. Amen.

TESTIMONY

We have the privilege of spending time with many children who live on the streets. Most of these children carry a very heavy burden. They have little or no family, they have no money, and they have no place to rest. They carry burdens that many of us will never know, although some of us have experienced such burdens and do understand these children's plight. These are precious children; it is vital for them to understand that Christ wants to carry their burdens for them.

Our time with these children is spent loving them, hugging them, talking with them, eating with them, and praying with them. One of the most frequent prayers we pray over these children is a prayer of thanks. Even though their current circumstances may be very difficult, we can praise God that He created each child to be special and has a great plan for each of their lives.

As we thank and praise God for His purposes for the children, we are always amazed to see their countenances change. We watch many of their burdens being lifted right off of them when suddenly they realize that God has a special purpose for each of them. Their perspectives change from visions of gloom to the awareness of light!

We haven't seen anything more powerful or effective in these children's lives than when we thank God for the plan He has ahead for them. Now, instead of focusing on the burdens they had always borne, they are free to dream about God's purpose for their lives and to thank Him for His plan for them.

APPLICATION

Find one person with whom you can pray through and complete the following steps:

- Take your Bible with you.
- Go out into the public areas near you where you know there are people in need. This might be the streets, the marketplace, around a café, or another area of town.

- Ask God to show you whom He wants to minister to during this time.

- Approach the person He shows you. Introduce yourself and find out what her name is.

- Ask her what is going on in her life.

- Ask how you can pray for her.

- Ask her to name one thing in her life for which she is thankful.

- Share with her one thing for which you are thankful to God.

- Invite her to spend time in prayer with you, thanking God for these things.

- When you pray with her, be sure to thank and praise God for His special plan for her life.

- Remind her to continue thanking God and assure her that you will be praying for the rest of her needs.

- Thank the person for sharing her life and time; thank her also for trusting God with you.

- Tell her good-bye, using her name, as this imputes value.

BEFORE YOU GO

Wait on the Lord

Once again, before you go out, remember this most important part: before we can walk with Jesus or be like Jesus to others, we must first spend time with Jesus. Find a quiet place to be alone with God. Ask Him to change you and your heart. Ask Him to help you see His children as He sees them. Allow the Holy Spirit to fill you and direct you. He is your Teacher and your Helper. Jesus said that it was to our advantage that He went away because He would send His Spirit to help us in all things (see John 16:7, 13-14). Wait on the Lord and allow the Holy Spirit to prepare you for the ways in which He is calling you to join Him.

STEP 3

Let the oppressed go free (Isaiah 58:6 NKJV).

EXPLANATION

Do you hear what God is saying? Free! God wants to free those who are captive to the world and its ways. In the last step, we looked at undoing the heavy burdens that depress people. In this call from the Lord, we must believe God for the oppressed to be set free. The definition of oppress is: "to burden with cruel or unjust… restraints; subject to a burdensome or harsh exercise of authority or power…"[1]

The enemy uses the world to be cruel, burdensome, unjust, restraining, and harsh to God's people. Here in Ethiopia, much oppression comes from poverty, but the enemy will oppress with anything he can find to keep us from walking in God's power. Is it any wonder that Jesus spent so much time during His ministry setting the oppressed free? When Jesus began His ministry, He read a passage from Isaiah 61:1-2 about His calling, a mission that we are now called to join Him in:

The Spirit of the Lord GOD is upon Me, because the LORD has anointed Me to preach good tidings to the poor; He has sent Me to heal the brokenhearted, to proclaim liberty to the captives, and the opening of the prison to those who are bound; to proclaim the acceptable year of the LORD... (NKJV).

The enemy uses the world to apply pressure that is designed to keep us from being free to live the lives for which God created us. Sometimes we submit ourselves willingly to those pressures, and sometimes they find us when we least expect them.

Either way, we are called to help free those who are held captive by oppression. Jesus is the way, the truth, and the life (see John 14:6). He is the door to freedom! If we will trust God, we can help the oppressed around us to trust God as He shows them His way out.

PRAYER

Lord Jesus, I want to be more like You. Please forgive me for the ways I have protected self and help me to fulfill my call to free the captives. Lord, please enlighten my eyes; help me to see. Please increase my faith, strengthen my love and help me to walk with You, Jesus, in compassion, truth, and grace. It is in Jesus's name I pray. Amen!

TESTIMONY

When we talk to the street kids with whom we work, one of the greatest needs they express involves the poverty that oppresses them. We always share with them promises from the Bible that talk about God as our provider. But then we take time to tell them stories from our own family about how God has faithfully provided for us during our greatest times of need. Then we pray with them to help show them how to trust God. Many people need to be shown, not just told.

Right now, there are many "street mothers" begging for money in one particular area. Their young children are learning to take on the same oppression that their moms are walking in. We can tell them how to get out and we can give them money, but neither is a long-term fix. Instead, Alex has been meeting with the moms asking what they need. They don't just ask for money; they want jobs. We have prayed with some moms and presented them with the possibility of having their own businesses on the streets. They have loved this idea!

However, we didn't have the money and neither did they. We knew God was working in this and wanted us to trust Him, so Alex asked them to pray and trust God with us, believing for Him to provide. Some of these street mothers were from different religious backgrounds, but all committed to trust God and all began praying. The best part is that after six weeks of praying and trusting God, our prayers were answered! God provided for these mothers to exit their oppression and start new paths in business. We didn't provide for them, God did! All we did was trust God along with them.

Those who are oppressed by the world need more than to hear about the way out; they need to be shown how to trust God.

APPLICATION

Find one person with whom you can pray through and complete the following steps:

- Go out into the public areas near you where you know there are people in need. This might be the streets, the marketplace, around a café, or another area of town.

- Ask God to show you an oppressed person to whom He wants to minister during this time.

- Approach the person He shows you. Introduce yourself and find out what his name is.

- Ask him what is going on in his life.

- Share with him your testimony of how Jesus saved you, freed you, provided for you, or healed you.

- Share with him Jesus's story, as well as His promises regarding the truth and grace He has given.

- Ask him if you can pray for him and his circumstances.

- Gently lay your hand on him and hold him up to the Lord in prayer.

- After you finish praying over him, ask him whether he will trust God with you to find His help.

- Ask him whether he knows Jesus or would like to know Him.

- If he would like to know Jesus, help him pray with you to know Jesus both as his Savior and as the Lord of his life.

- Whether you take the previous step or not, thank the person for sharing his life and time; thank him also for trusting God with you.

- As you say good-bye, let him know you will continue to pray for him, and remind him to continue to pray as well.

BEFORE YOU GO

Wait on the Lord

As you spend this time with God, take a few moments to remember all that He has done for you. Make sure that the testimony of Jesus is fresh and alive in your heart and mind. Seek the Lord with passion and desire, read His Word, and allow Him to speak into your heart. Don't just pray, but seek Him and allow God to touch you with His presence. God's promises are great to those who wait on Him! Enjoy your time with the Lord.

STEP 4

Break every [enslaving] yoke (Isaiah 58:6 AMP).

EXPLANATION

This verse represents the worldly attachments we build in our lives. Unfortunately, many of our attachments are not of God. We become yoked, or attached, to many different things, people, and actions in this world that separate us from God. These unhealthy yokes oppress us, depress us, and weigh us down. We cannot expect to go forward while still attached to the yokes this world offers. God says we, His people, are called to break these yokes.

Specifically, look at the word *enslaving* from the Amplified Version of the Bible. Most of us do not realize that our worldly attachments are more than just bad habits or wrong patterns; instead, they are actual ties that enslave us and limit us to lives that are less than God's best. These enslaving yokes must be broken!

Have you ever known someone who is addicted to something? The obvious addictions are things like poverty, alcohol, drugs, sexual habits, and other issues that are easy to see on the surface. Many of us, however, are enslaved by or addicted to things that are often less apparent, such as anger, bitterness, insecurity, lies, the worshiping of false idols, and even demonic activity. These things keep us from seeing God correctly.

If those who are yoked or enslaved by the world are ever to know the truth Jesus called us to preach, we must first break any yokes in our lives and then help others break the yokes, addictions, and enslaving relationships that bind them. Remember, most people who are enslaved by the things of this world cannot see the prisons they are in. Their chains are not always obvious to the eye or to the touch. Their spiritual eyes must be opened. We do this through prayer. We go before God on behalf of others to pray for them, and to intercede for their release from that which binds them. We call upon our loving God, whose love does not fail, and who is able to do much more than we can ever imagine (see Eph. 3:20). We pray, and we believe! We believe, and we pray! We trust God that through our prayers He is able to break any and every enslaving yoke that binds people from coming into a personal relationship with Jesus Christ.

PRAYER

Lord Jesus, I know there are so many people in this world, people just outside of where I am right now, who are yoked to the world. Lord, I may not be able to join You in breaking every yoke, but I ask You to show me those to whom You are calling me. Please give me wisdom and discernment. Please give me revelation directly from You, Lord. Even now I pray for those to whom You are calling me. Please increase my love and faith for them. I believe You, God! Please teach me how to join You and teach me how to pray. In Jesus's name we pray. Amen.

TESTIMONY

Recently, we had the privilege of spending a great deal of time with a little boy who had experienced a lot of trauma from the world in his young life. He had brain damage, was born two months early, and his arms and legs shook rapidly in panic every couple of minutes. He had been abandoned on the side of the road, and you could still see the fear and desperation he had suffered. He could not make eye contact, could barely eat, and never showed a smile. He was yoked in infirmity, fear, and past experiences, and seemed unaware of what was going on around him.

Nevertheless, the Lord told us to pray. God spoke to our hearts His desire to break every one of these yokes. Every day we prayed for this precious but troubled little boy. We asked God for wisdom and for revelation from the Holy Spirit. One Saturday, we felt led by God to pray over this little boy and believe God to begin to break the yokes of the world. First, we waited on God. We asked God to teach us how to pray to see these yokes broken and asked Him which Bible promises we were to pray during that time. Then we gathered as a family around the boy and laid hands on him. We prayed exactly as the Lord instructed us to and believed God to do the rest. We believed that God would break every yoke on his behalf.

We finished the prayer time and were amazed! The little boy stopped crying in terror, he made eye contact with us for the first time, and he even began to smile. His fearful shaking began to stop and he started to look around the room as if he were observing life for the first time. God broke the yokes!

The next day we had another prayer time over the boy, asking God to pour back His wholeness into the places where the little boy had been yoked to the world. We asked God to heal him. We asked Him to fill the fearful places with love and the wounded places with hope. We asked God to give this little boy what only He could give him. Once again, we saw an amazing change after this prayer time: The little boy's tense body began to relax, and some of his physical infirmities began to change. God was healing him.

The next day, our friend, who was very close to this little boy, came over to visit us. We had not yet told her what God had done. She spent some time with the little boy and came over after a little while. "He is so different," she said. "What happened? He just seems so different now."

We could tell her nothing except that God had released him, broken the yokes of the world, and had begun a great healing in the boy. God wants to do the same thing for other captives.

APPLICATION

Find one person with whom you can pray through and complete the following steps:

- Go out into the public areas near you where you know there are people in need. This might be the streets, the marketplace, around a café, or another area of town.

- Ask the Lord to cover you in the armor of God (see Eph. 6:10-17) and in humility. Begin to praise Him for all He will do.

- Ask God to show you whom He wants to minister to during this time. Is there a person or a group of people God may be leading you to pray for?

- Ask God to show you how He sees this person or people. Ask God to teach you His love for them.

- From wherever you and your prayer partner sit, begin to pray for this person or group of people. Ask God to reveal to you the bondages that might be enslaving them. Is it poverty? Sickness? Some other yoke of bondage?

- Pray with your prayer partner. Keep praying in love for the person or group God has shown you. Pray until He tells you to stop.

- After you leave this place today, continue to pray and intercede for those whom God revealed to you.

- Go with the same prayer partner to the same place and pray for this person or group of people again. Continue for as many days as you feel led.

- Now begin to pray for God to fill the old areas once yoked to the world with His love, grace, truth, faith, and whatever else He knows they need.

- When the Lord leads you to do so, go with your prayer partner to meet the person(s) you have been praying for. Introduce yourself and ask them their name(s).

- Ask the person or group of people what has been going on in their lives.

- Share your testimony about how God saved you.

- Tell this person or group of people about God's love, the Gospel of Jesus Christ, and the special plan God has for every life (see Jer. 29:11).

- Ask this person or people if you can pray over them now.

- Lay your hands on them and hold them to the Father in prayer.

- Believe God to do a work in their lives!

- Thank the person or group of people for sharing their lives and time; thank them also for trusting God with you.

- Tell them good-bye, addressing them by name, and remind them that you will continue to pray for them.

BEFORE YOU GO

Wait on the Lord

Before you start these steps, it is important that you continue to cultivate closeness with God. It is very difficult to join Him in His calling if you are not sensitive to how the Holy Spirit speaks His Word to your heart. Take 30 minutes or an hour to sit still and be alone with God. Draw near to Him and He promises to draw near to you (see James 4:8). Get to know God better so He can lead you in every little detail.

We can't be His sheep if we do not know His voice. We cannot know His voice if we do not take the time. Wait on the Lord and He promises you will not be ashamed.

STEP 5

Is it not to share your bread with the hungry? (Isaiah 58:7 NKJV).

EXPLANATION

Sharing food with the hungry is a necessary and powerful form of love. Before Jesus miraculously fed the 5,000 (see Matt. 14:21) and the 4,000 (see Matt. 15:38), the Bible says that He was moved with compassion (see Matt. 14:14; 15:32). Hunger can hurt. Sharing a meal with someone may seem like a basic thing to do, but it is true ministry in a very pure form. How often do we rely on God to meet our basic needs? Now we have the same opportunity to join Him in doing this for others. We must learn the same compassion Jesus felt before He provided for so many in this way. We must learn to love like Jesus did, and to love like Jesus still does.

Fasting from food is something we do often as Christians. There are many good motives for fasting, but there are also many times when we fast simply as a religious exercise. Isaiah 58:6 NKJV starts by declaring, *"Is this not the fast that I have chosen?"* As we have discussed earlier, this fast is not one from food, but a fast from self. It is a fast of love. So perhaps in looking to feed the hungry, we fast from our food in order to give our meals to those in need. In this we are not fasting for the sake of religion or self, but we are entering into a fast of love. It is a fast to show love toward God and for the purpose of loving others.

When looking to fulfill the call to share our food with the hungry, it is safe to say that many of us do not have the resources to freely or frequently give food to others. But if we combine our fasting that is meant for closeness with God with our feeding the hungry, we fulfill both of the two "great" commandments given by our Lord (see Matt. 22:35-39). Perhaps you and your family can fast from your lunch or dinner and package up the food you would have eaten to take to someone who is hungry. Or instead of going out for a meal, you could use the money you would have spent at a restaurant to buy the same meals in "to go" or "takeaway" packaging that you can easily deliver to others.

Ask the Lord to show you how to join Him in this great act of love. Let God open your eyes to those who are hungry; then live out this simple but powerful act of love. The hungry are everywhere, and we must do no less than share our bread with them. Is this not the fast that He has chosen?

PRAYER

Heavenly Father, You are my provider. I love You and want to love others like You do. Please help me to share my bread with the hungry as You share Your love and provision with me. Help me to know how to join You in their lives. Jesus, please teach me the same compassion that You had when You prayed over and distributed food to the multitudes. Lord, please use me as a vessel of love and provision for others. Help me to bless the hungry as You have blessed me. Thank You, Lord. I love You and I want to live out the true fast that You have chosen. In Jesus's name I pray. Amen.

TESTIMONY

One of the most enjoyable and memorable things God allows us to do each month is to go out to lunch with a group of children from the street. We sit down at a restaurant and are surrounded at the table by so many of these precious kids. All of the children are very hungry and eat quickly, but you can see that their true focus is on something more than the food: It's on the relationship of love that we are building together. During lunch we even feed one another hand to mouth, as is customary in the Ethiopian culture. The truly special thing is that the kids don't just want us to feed them; they want to feed us and have us share food *with* them.

Food is a powerful form of provision, but most of all, it is a symbol for the love and value that their hearts are hungering for. Sharing food with someone is an open door to share love, laughter, tears, prayer, and smiles. Giving someone food teaches them the principle of how God loves us, not only as our provider, but also as our Father. These kids teach us how to love like Jesus. They remind us of why Jesus lived and loved like He did while on Earth. We learn more about love every time we share one of these meals.

APPLICATION

Find one person with whom you can pray through and complete the following steps:

- Choose one meal to fast from together.

- Take the food or money you would have spent on that meal with you to feed the hungry.

- Go out into the public areas near you where you know there are people in need. This might be the streets, the marketplace, around a café, or another area of town.

- Ask God to show you who is hungry and in need of this act of love.

- Pray over the food or provision and bless it for His name's sake, as Jesus did before He fed the multitudes (see Matt. 14:19; 15:36).

- Approach the person(s) God has led you to. Ask them their name(s) and ask them if they would like some food.

- Offer the food or money that you brought and let the hungry know that it is from the Lord who loves them.

- Ask the person(s) if you can pray for them.

- Lay your hands on them and hold them up before the Father in prayer.

- Pray for God's provision in their lives.

- Remind them of God's promise from Matthew 5:6: *"Blessed are those who hunger and thirst for righteousness, for they will be filled."*

- Thank the person(s) for their time and remind them of Jesus's love for them.

- Tell the person(s) good-bye, addressing them by name, and continue to pray for them.

BEFORE YOU GO

Wait on the Lord

As we have discussed in each step, this part is very important. We cannot fully show God's love to others if we have not spent time with Jesus ourselves. Find a place to be alone with Him. Take this time to develop your hunger for more of God and more of His love. Express this hunger to Him in prayer and by faith expect that He will fill you. As you spend time with Jesus, ask Him to make your compassion like His. Ask Him to increase your faith and to multiply His love through you to others. Spend this time with God and let the Holy Spirit fill you up in preparation for taking this step.

STEP 6

Bring to your house the poor who are cast out (Isaiah 58:7 NKJV).

EXPLANATION

Millions of people in this world lack shelter. Many of our friends and many of the children we love have been cast out of their homes, which is in part how we came to know and love them.

Homelessness has many causes; some are self-inflicted and some result from difficult circumstances. The bottom line is this: Whatever the reason for their homelessness, everyone who is poor or cast out needs redemption in this area of their lives!

This is an issue that causes much fear for many people. Fear often rises when we consider bringing into our homes people we do not know. This is a natural feeling, but not necessarily a godly feeling. Regardless of our fears, God wants us to bring into our homes those who are cast out.

We are really working on this in our family. As with anything, we need to use wisdom and discernment, but we should not automatically deny the possibility of offering this kind of love simply because we are afraid. If we allow fear to control us, the enemy wins. God's love is greater and more perfect than any fear. To provide shelter for someone who is cast out is an amazing act of love, as the person can then experience God's love in every aspect of the new comfort that now surrounds them.

Not everyone has a home or the circumstances necessary to take in the outcast. But even if you do not have this freedom, you might know someone who does; or you might know of someplace where shelter is available. Many cities offer assistance of this kind. Perhaps there is an inexpensive motel room nearby. Or, maybe God has given you everything you need to bring someone in need into your home.

There are a variety of approaches to loving others in this way. We just need to act in love, obedience, and faith. We must be prayerful and align ourselves with the Word of God. Sometimes, we might have to be creative!

If you seek God for shelter for someone in need, He will show you how to provide it in the best way possible. Anything is possible with God, just ask Him! (See Mark 10:27; James 4:2.)

PRAYER

Lord, I need Your help. I want to fulfill Your Word, but I am afraid and don't always know how. Would You please show me how to love others in this way? Help me to bring into shelter those who are cast out. Show me the right person or people. Please provide what is necessary as only You can. Please guard and protect me as I step with You in this. Give me Your wisdom and discernment. Teach me Your ways in this, Holy Spirit. Please bless someone else with the love, mercy, and shelter that they need. In Jesus's name I pray. Amen.

TESTIMONY

This part of Isaiah 58 remains very close to our hearts. When we first arrived in Ethiopia, we stayed in a guest house for three weeks before moving into our home. We had taken two trips to Ethiopia before moving here and had met many wonderful people from many different backgrounds.

One of the people we met halfway through our first trip was Alex. Alex had lived in a plastic house on the street since the age of seven, shining shoes to make money. A close friend and mission partner here in Addis Ababa introduced us to him as they had been close for many years. Alex's dad died when he was only two years old and his mom remarried when he was seven. At that time, she was asked by her husband to leave her family behind; this meant that seven-year-old Alex was left on the street.

Alex lived on the street on and off for many of the next 16 years of his life. He found the Lord, but still struggled to find God's path for his life. He did amazingly well for someone who had lived through so much; it was clear that God had a special plan for his life.

During our first week after we moved into our home, God began speaking to our hearts about Alex. We felt very strongly that he was to move into our home and live with us as family. He was 23 at the time and sleeping wherever he could. We prayed and talked to those we trusted and felt that this was of God. Alex indeed moved into our home and became part of our family.

Alex has lived with us for almost two years now and his place in the family continues to grow. Our mom is his mom, our sister his sister, and so on. Alex now walks in Jesus's steps in an amazing way, helping us to live out Isaiah 58 across the city. He prays with many kids, helps children and families who are in need, and has three weekly Bible studies and prayer times with between 40 and 50 children from the street each week.

God had a special plan for Alex's life all along, but he needed a home. God gave him a home and now God is using Alex to give love and life in Jesus Christ to many others! We are so proud of Alex and blessed by what God has done in all our lives.

APPLICATION

- Spend time in prayer with your family, those in your home, or a close friend and prayer partner.

- Ask God to show you someone who is poor and cast out and who needs to be brought in for shelter.

- Go out with your prayer partner(s) into the public areas, the streets, and the marketplaces. Pray as you walk.

- Ask God to show you someone who has been cast out and needs shelter. (Perhaps it is someone you already know; maybe it is someone new. The next steps are dependent upon the circumstances in your lives and the life of the person you are called to help.)

- Spend time praying for this person and ask God how you are to help her find shelter. Take your time so that you make a godly decision.

- You could take her to a nearby homeless shelter.

- You could take her to a facility that offers inexpensive housing.

- You could begin a relationship with her, getting to know her and praying for her as you consider the possibility of bringing her into your home, or somewhere else that is more suitable.

- Seek the help, prayers, and wisdom of others whom you trust.

- Get to know the person, learn her story, feed her, and pray over her.

- Make no promises to her until God has made it abundantly clear to you what He desires for you to do in regard to her shelter.

- Take her to whatever place of shelter He shows you. Your next steps should be prayerful and loving. These steps will depend upon the circumstances surrounding everyone involved.

- Make sure she knows that this shelter is provided by the grace and love of God.

BEFORE YOU GO!

Wait on the Lord

Before you go out, continue in your time alone with the Lord. The more time you spend with Him, the more your actions will reflect Him. Be still before God and let Him fill you up. Allow Him to increase your faith. Allow God to increase your love. Inquire of the Lord as to how, where, when, and with whom you are to join Him in these steps. Wait on God until He sends you out into His steps. Go with love!

STEP 7

When you see the naked…cover him (Isaiah 58:7 NKJV).

EXPLANATION

My heart breaks to think of those who are without clothes to cover themselves. We walk and drive past many people each day who have very little, and oftentimes nothing to cover themselves. Men, women, children, nursing mothers, people of all ages and circumstances surround us and wait in need. What a simple but powerful way to show someone Jesus's love.

We believe that many people must be shown love before they can receive the truth that we give them. Covering those who are naked, or those who have similar needs is something all of us can do for those around us. They may not be sitting in the street completely unclothed, but this does not mean that they are completely warm. My heart breaks even now to think about the number of people I have walked or driven by who needed something that I have—clothes.

Some of us have old clothes and some have resources available to buy new clothes for others. Even an extra blanket from home would be a tremendous blessing for someone in need. In a similar way to what we discussed in regard to feeding the hungry, we can fast for a couple of meals during the week and use the money saved to buy warm clothing for someone who needs it.

The biggest thing we must remember is that we are called to cover the naked when we see them, but we will not see them unless we take the time to look. As you take this step of love and faith, know that this provision will meet a very real need; but even more, the love that you show will warm someone's heart and prepare a place for the Lord.

PRAYER

Lord Jesus, I want to see others through Your eyes of love. I want to have Your compassion and show Your love to others by walking in the faith You have called me to. Please help me. I want to be more like You, and this includes covering those who are naked. Lord, would You please provide all that is necessary for me to join You in this way? Please help me to love my neighbors as myself. It is in Jesus's name I pray. Amen.

TESTIMONY

Something we practice is to look through all our family's old clothes and give them to Alex, who then finds people on the streets who need them. Sometimes we purchase blankets and together take them out either early in the morning or late in the evening to find those who have a genuine need. Alex always looks for someone who might need a pair of shoes, then comes and asks us whether it is OK to give the person his own shoes. "Of course, however God leads you to give," we remind him. Then he takes some time to pray and to ask God.

No matter what the Lord gives us to cover others or how often we have done so, I will never forget the time that I did not. It was our first trip to Ethiopia. We were staying in a local guest house and met someone there who once lived in Addis Ababa. He wanted to take me out late that night to show me his practice of distributing bread to the hungry. There were three of us in the car, and we stopped each time we found someone or a group of people who might be hungry.

As we drove away from one of the last groups of men we found sleeping on the street, I noticed that one of them was completely naked. All of them were in need of more covering, but this man had nothing. The car was already in motion when I realized what I should have done; I should have taken off my shirt at that very moment and handed it to him. Instead, I hesitated and missed the opportunity to cover this man and fulfill God's call. I think back to that scene often. I still think I should have taken off my shirt for him; I still grieve to remember that I did not. Next time I will stop the car and take the shirt off my own back, knowing that I have plenty more in my closet at home.

I don't want to have any more regrets like this one. As a family, we do our best to take time and resources to clothe the naked, but it is an area in which we need to improve.

APPLICATION

Find one person with whom you can pray through and complete the following steps:

- Take at least one clothing item or blanket in a bag with you. This can be from your own home or something that you purchase new. If you are skilled at sewing, consider making an article of clothing or a blanket.

- Go out into the public areas near you where you know there are people in need. This might be the streets, the marketplace, around a café, or another area of town.

- Ask God to show you whom He wants to minister to during this time.

- Approach the person He shows you. Introduce yourself and find out what his name is.

- Ask him what is going on in his life.

- Tell him about your love for Jesus and what He has done in your life.

- Offer him the covering you have brought for him. Let him know that this gift has come by way of God's love.

- Ask him whether he would allow you to pray over him.

- Lay your hands on him and lift him up to the Lord in prayer. Pray for God's full love, hope, and faith to be in this person's heart, and for God's covering to be over him.

- Thank him for his time and for sharing his life with you.

- Tell him good-bye, addressing him by name, and let him know that you will be praying for him. Fulfill your commitment by continuing in prayer for him on your own.

BEFORE YOU GO

Wait on the Lord

We believe the best way to become more like someone is to spend more time with that person. If we truly want to live more like Jesus, then we must take more time with Him. Set aside 45 minutes or an hour to be alone with God. Talk to Him, thank Him, praise Him, read His Word, and be still so you can listen to Him. Allow the Lord to mold you in His image and prepare you to love as He loves.

The more time you spend with God, the more others will see and feel His love and light from your life when you go out into the streets and marketplaces with Him.

STEP 8

Take away the yoke from your midst, the pointing of the finger, and speaking wickedness (Isaiah 58:9 NKJV).

EXPLANATION

Years ago, this was the first part of Isaiah 58 I began praying about in my own life. In the Bible, Jesus speaks specifically about judging one another, reminding us that the measure we apply to others will also be applied back to us (see Matt. 7:2).

Isaiah 58:9 talks about the yoke we often live with that causes us to be critical, judgmental, and negative in our perspective of others. Oftentimes, we feel so poorly about ourselves or fear the judgment of people to such an extent that we criticize others to protect ourselves. This is a yoke that has become far too common and accepted in the world around us. We must be very intentional in love and in resisting criticism in order to see this yoke removed from our lives.

Although this step from Isaiah 58 is not necessarily an action step in the streets, it is vital to our ability to walk with the Lord through any of the other steps by which He has called us to follow Him. The only way we can walk in and offer the love and mercy shown in Isaiah 58 is to see others through God's perspective instead of through judgment and criticism.

If we take this step to see this destructive yoke removed from our lives, we will not only see our lives changed, but the Lord also will be able to use us to have a more profound and loving impact on others. It is because of judgments in our lives that many of us do not go out to the needy and the poor in the streets and marketplaces. Many of us fear and judge the people who need love the most. We have built up false perspectives that keep us from joining God in His harvest fields!

If we will remove these yokes from our midst—whether accusation, criticism or judgment—and replace these perspectives with God's eyes of love, we will begin to see the paths and purposes God has set out before us. As we become free from these yokes, we will be able to love as Jesus loves and reach out with Him toward all who cross our paths.

PRAYER

Lord Jesus, please help me to see others through Your eyes of love and mercy. Please cleanse me of my judgments, accusations, and criticisms of others. Instead of looking for what is wrong, please help me to look for what is right. Please replace these things in my life with more of Your faith in others, hope for Your purpose in their lives, and love for who You have made them to be. Lord, I resist this yoke of judgment and criticism, and it must flee from my life. Lord Jesus, I surrender to Your perspective. Thank You for teaching me to see as You see. It is in Jesus's name I pray. Amen.

TESTIMONY

One thing that we seek to practice often is prayer walking. It can be a great way to get out and spend time alone with God, yet it also puts you out in public where you can pray about what God is doing. This is also one of our favorite ways to practice love.

If I ever find myself feeling anything less than love for others, I know it is the perfect time for a prayer walk. As I walk, I ask the Lord to teach me how He sees those around me. I make eye contact with those who walk past me; I offer a smile and a respectful nod. I ask God who I can pray for and I look for ways to love them. My goal is to walk around with my heart wide-eyed at God's potential in others. I want to walk with compassion, mercy, humility, and love. This is not always easy, but it is the goal.

To see others through God's eyes became such a goal for me that I embarked on an unusual fast a number of years ago. I fasted from wearing sunglasses. Now, I understand that sunglasses do not limit my sight in this way. I understand that they do not change how I see someone or love someone, and I realize that it may sound like a funny thing to do.

But my prayer at that time was that nothing would keep me from seeing others the way God sees them. I did not want my perspective to be hindered in even the slightest way, as I knew this was the kind of love God wanted from me. Though sunglasses do not hinder me from seeing others as God sees them, they are designed to shade my view of that which is bright. Therefore, the fast was a symbolic one.

By not wearing sunglasses for a year, I reminded myself daily that I did not want anything to change my vision in an adverse way. I did not want to view anyone in less light than God created them to be seen in. By fasting in this way, I devoted myself to seeing everyone in light rather than darkness. Everyone has been created in God's image, and though people sometimes choose to walk in darkness, they still have light deep down inside them waiting to come out.

I wanted to see God's light in others and to use love to help draw out that light. Sometimes our perspective becomes shaded, critical, or judgmental. I wanted to be freed of this yoke so that I could live, love, and find light in others the way Jesus would. It was a much-needed change in perspective.

APPLICATION

Find one person with whom you can pray through and complete the following steps:

- Spend time in prayer together, asking God to teach you His love and His perspective.

- Repent before the Lord of any judgment, criticism, bitterness, accusation, or lack of love that may be in your heart toward others.

- Ask God to refill these places with more faith, hope, and love.

- Go out into the public areas near you where you know there are people in need. This might be the streets, the marketplace, around a café, or another area of town.

- Practice seeing with God's eyes by praying for those in need around you. The more you pray for them, the easier it is to see them as Jesus does.

- Ask God to point out one person near you.

- How do you think God sees her? What do you think His perspective is—not of her actions, but of her heart?

- Pray for the person. Ask God to help her be the person God has created her to be. Pray about God's purposes in her life.

- Approach this person and give her some simple encouragement. Perhaps you could say, "I just wanted to tell you that God loves you and has a special plan for your life."

- If led to, continue the conversation by learning her story and how you can pray for her. Make sure she understands that she is special and is loved by God.

- Ask her if you can pray over her right there.

- Lay hands on the person and hold her up to God in prayer, asking Him to meet her and to help her fulfill His purpose for her life.

- Thank her for sharing her life and time; thank her also for trusting God with you.

- Tell her good-bye, addressing her by name, and tell her that you will continue to pray for her.

BEFORE YOU GO

Wait on the Lord

What has helped the most in our desire to see others as God sees them is our time spent waiting on Him in prayer. When we meditate on the Word of God and spend time with Him, we are refreshed and receive new perspectives toward the people and the world around us.

Take this time in prayer to be still with God. Allow the Holy Spirit to fill you with His love. Allow God to transform these parts of your life by surrendering to Him. Seek after the Lord until you experience His presence around you. This may take time, but we must learn to experience God if we want to experience others the way He does. Enjoy your time with the Lord.

STEP 9

Extend your soul to the hungry (Isaiah 58:10 NKJV).

EXPLANATION

The thing I love about this verse is the word *soul*. This calling from the Lord does not simply exhort us to extend our food to the hungry, but to extend our souls to the hungry. The soul is one of the innermost, deepest parts of us, and God is calling us to extend it to others.

It is a great and powerful thing to give food to those in need, but how much more impactful would it be to offer *ourselves?* Self is what often keep us from walking as Jesus walked. Self makes us fear, it makes us proud, and it makes us want in selfish ways. It is when we deny self that we have something extra to extend to others. There are millions of hungry people in this world, but how many more people need something beyond mere food?

If I am going to extend from my soul, what shall I give? If it comes from the soul, it must be something of meaning. It is in the soul that we treasure what is most valuable to us, whether money or time, or a practical or spiritual gift that God has given us to share with others. We must pray about the deep and treasured parts of our lives that God may want to take to others. What has God entrusted us with? What do we hold most dear? How can we share this treasure with others? If God has freely given it to us, how can we not freely offer it to others? (See Matthew 10:8.)

PRAYER

Lord God, You have entrusted me with something that You want to share with others. Please show me what You have put in my life that I can offer to those in need. Lord, I give You all that I hold most dear and ask that You would be glorified through it. Please show me how to extend my soul to those in need. Please give me the faith to give freely with You. I want to trust You with all my heart, to lean not on my own understanding, and in all my ways to acknowledge You. I know You will direct my paths.² I surrender to You, Lord, I surrender all! I love You. In Jesus's name I pray. Amen.

TESTIMONY

God has told us to open our home to others. God has filled our home with family and friends. Alex moved in from the streets; the Lord had us take care of a foster baby for six months; and by the grace of God, we have had the privilege of adopting two children. We are always stretched by extending this part of our soul, but we are more blessed by the people God has brought into our lives through such giving.

Our house has been continuously if not overly full. We never know when a child from the orphanage may come to stay a few nights, or when God might bring someone else in need. But we have learned that as much as we would sometimes relish the selfish desire for our home to be an uneventful haven for us, God has better plans and has asked us to make it available to others. It can be exhausting, but it is never a burden. Why? If we are joining the Lord in extending our souls, He gives us all the grace we need to fulfill such giving. He never said it would not be hard, but He does promise that it is worth it!

It would be easy to protect our home in an effort to maintain a calm and peaceful place for our family; but if we did so, we would miss out on so much that the Lord has to offer, both to us and to others. By extending this part of our souls, God has added to our family, and we have been richly blessed!

APPLICATION

Find one person with whom you can pray through and complete the following steps:

- In prayer, ask God to show you what He has given you that you can offer to others.

- Go out into the public areas, streets, marketplaces, cafés, etc., and pray for those in need.

- What do you have in your soul that might help meet a need among those around you?

- Perhaps God will first show you what you have to give, or maybe He will begin by showing you to whom He asks that you extend yourself.

- What is it that God wants to extend from your life to others?

- With whom does He want to share this part of your life?

- Spend time in prayer and ask God to show you how to extend this part of your life to the person or group that is in need.

- Make any preparations the Lord speaks to you about.

- Approach the person or people, introduce yourself, and ask them their names.

- Ask questions to find out about their lives and/or their needs.

- Any additional steps in regard to these people and needs will depend upon what the Lord has shown you He wants to extend to others through your life.

- It may take time to build the relationships necessary to extend yourself to specific individuals or groups. God may have something specific for you to give them, or your part may simply be to pray. Whatever it is, make sure you ask the Lord for His direction and timing; this will enable you to show the person or group of people His love.

BEFORE YOU GO

Wait on the Lord

As we have discussed throughout each step, this part of the process is powerful. When we learn to wait on the Lord, we take the time to listen to God and to receive direction from Him. When we know how to listen to His voice and His Word in our hearts, we also know how to obey Him. If, in faith, we obey what the Lord speaks to us, then we need only trust Him to bring it all together in His timing. Take this time to be still with God. What is He saying to you? How is He leading your heart? Let Him fill you up to be prepared for this step. Listen to Him! Obey Him! Trust Him!

STEP 10

Satisfy the needs of the oppressed (Isaiah 58:10).

EXPLANATION

Are we truly able to satisfy someone else's need? The word *satisfy* creates a very large task, one that is much bigger than what we usually do, and one that we cannot do on our own. The promise from God's Word that immediately comes to heart is one Jesus spoke in Matthew 19:26: *"With man this is impossible, but with God all things are possible."*

Do you believe this promise to be true? I do, but my actions do not always confirm that I believe it! My love and faith should cause me to obediently join God in actions that are bigger than self, therefore causing me to trust Him to do what I cannot. I ought to love the Lord and my neighbors to the extent that I must overstep my own reality and enter into the reality of faith. It is easy to say we believe all things are possible with God; it is another thing to live like we believe all things are possible with God.

We have discussed the needs of the oppressed extensively in the previous steps and have identified many oppressed people who may live near us. Now we must ask God to teach us how to satisfy their needs. This will require an act of faith based on a motive of love. It is very important to remember that Jesus's promise does not say that anything is possible *for* God. Jesus's promise says that anything is possible *with* God! There is a big difference between doing something for God and doing it with Him.

If we are to see God's fruit in our lives, we must learn how to join Him where He is moving. We must make sure that we learn closeness with God to such an extent that we can discern whether our actions are based on *self* or on His leading. We must not go out determined to give to others and then ask God to bless our ministry. Rather, we must ask God to show us where He is moving and then take an obedient step of love and faith with Him. Jesus did nothing of Himself; He only did what He saw the Father doing (see John 5:19).

If we are to satisfy the needs of the oppressed, we must give them something bigger than ourselves, something they cannot give themselves. We must learn to give others even what we do not have by trusting in our God, who is able to do exceedingly and abundantly above all we could ask or think (see Eph. 3:20). He is able!

PRAYER

Lord, please increase my faith and teach me to know You more. Please teach me how to join You where You are moving and to see Your infinite possibilities by moving with You. God, You are more faithful than I know. Please help me to trust You more and to offer others what only You can give them. I cannot do this on my own, Lord. The only way anyone can be satisfied is if they receive something directly from You. Lord, please help me; Holy Spirit, please fill me. Please make me a vessel so full of You that I am overflowing to others. It is in Jesus's name I pray. Amen.

TESTIMONY

One of our favorite testimonies about trusting God to satisfy the needs of others is found in the Book of Acts. We have seen God move like this in a variety of ways, but this story from Acts 3:1-10 is a perfect example of what God is calling all of us to do:

Now Peter and John went up together to the temple at the hour of prayer, the ninth hour. And a certain man lame from his mother's womb was carried, whom they laid daily at the gate of the temple which is called Beautiful, to ask alms from those who entered the temple; who, seeing Peter and John about to go into the temple, asked for alms. And fixing his eyes on him, with John, Peter said, "Look at us." So he gave them his attention, expecting to receive something from them. Then Peter said, "Silver and gold I do not have, but what I do have I give you: In the name of Jesus Christ of Nazareth, rise up and walk." And he took him by the right hand and lifted him up, and immediately his feet and ankle bones received strength. So he, leaping up, stood and walked and entered the temple with them—walking, leaping, and praising God. And all the people saw him walking and praising God. Then they knew that it was he who sat begging alms at the Beautiful Gate of the temple; and they were filled with wonder and amazement at what had happened to him (Acts 3:1-10 NKJV).

I love how Peter and John handled this! Even though this needy and lame man put his expectation on them, they did not take on the burden personally. Instead, they immediately put their faith in God to satisfy the man's need. Peter and John's love and faith acted as a link between God and the man, whose need had not been satisfied since birth. He had never been able to care for himself and was forced to beg for provision. Instead of giving him that day's provision, they sought God for His "impossible" answer—a life completely transformed. Because they looked to Him and not themselves, they saw God deliver!

Many times, we enter such situations preempting God's answer by trying to do for the person in need whatever is in our human power to accomplish. What if God wants to do more? His Word makes it clear that He intends to satisfy the needs of the oppressed. Therefore, we know that we can trust God in the same way that John and Peter trusted Him. How exciting! John and Peter's faith in God's ability to answer helped satisfy the lame man's needs. Also, their faith inspired the people who had gathered around them as each had the privilege of watching God move.

John and Peter did not physically possess what this man really needed. But they did have faith—their faith in God's ability to satisfy allowed the lame man to receive what they could not personally give. John and Peter became the pipeline of love and faith through which God poured out His provision to another.

God wants to use us the same way.

APPLICATION

Each of the previous applications has been in a practical, step-by-step format. This time, however, the application is to pray and ask God to reveal the steps in which He desires you to join Him. If we are to offer others that which will satisfy, it will have to be given by God and put in order by Him. This requires us to be sensitive to the Holy Spirit; we need to ask Him to teach us how to do this. There are no "set" steps for this application, but if you will take the time and put your faith in Him who is able, He will show you what to do.

God will show you when He wants to move in this way. He will show you where He wants to move. The Lord will direct you to whomever He wants to satisfy; and if you will listen to Him and obey, He will show you how He wants to give something that is impossible for man to give, but is possible with God. God has moved in this way before, and He wants to show Himself through you again.

The application in this step is to apply our attention to the Lord as we go out and wait for Him to prompt our hearts to join Him. Walk in faith! Walk in love! Listen, obey, and then trust Him!

BEFORE YOU GO

Wait on the Lord

If we are to learn to hear the Lord's promptings in our hearts, we must practice this time with Him. We must take time to know our shepherd's voice and understand His ways. Open your Bible to the Gospels and read about Jesus. Meditate on the Lord and where He walked, how He loved, who He ministered to, and what He required. Be still before the Lord in prayer and ask Him to make you more like Him. Allow Him to prepare you, to teach you, to fill you; learn to listen for and heed the Holy Spirit's promptings in your heart. Enjoy your time with the Lord!

STEP 11

Turn away your foot from the Sabbath, from doing your pleasure on My holy day, and call the Sabbath a delight (Isaiah 58:13 NKJV).

EXPLANATION

We often feel compelled to keep going, keep ministering, and keep reacting to the fast-moving world around us. But taking a sabbath rest is a proactive step toward increasing love. Sometimes we find it easier to keep moving rather than to be still and allow God to move. However, our ability to fulfill God's call of love in Isaiah 58 is directly related to our ability to take this sabbath rest each and every week.

God's rest releases joy in our lives, and the Word of God tells us in Nehemiah 8:10 that *"the joy of the LORD is [our] strength"* (NKJV). We do not just want to fulfill the steps of Isaiah 58 as if we are crossing them off a list. We must live out this love toward others joyfully! The joy that is found in loving others is impossible to enjoy without knowing the sabbath rest of the Lord. When we rest in the Lord, we are refilled. When we are refilled, we are prepared and equipped. When we are prepared, we are ready for God to lead us in His ways.

The steps of Jesus are not easy; they require a love that goes far beyond self. This is a love that we cannot maintain on our own, a love that only He can reenergize in us. When we dismiss sabbath rest in our lives, we begin to rely on self, and self cannot sustain or multiply what God wants to do in and through our lives. We must cease from our works so God can do even greater works. We must turn our feet back to the Sabbath so Jesus can lead us in His steps.

PRAYER

Lord my God, thank You! Thank You for wanting this Sabbath time with me and for allowing it in my life.

Please help me take the time to rest with You so that I can receive Your strength to live out Your steps, Jesus. I want to love like You love, and I cannot do this from my own strength. Lord, I need what only You can give. Please help me to make myself still before You and to use our time of rest together for Your love and glory. Thank You, Lord! It is in Jesus's name I pray. Amen.

TESTIMONY

When I was 17, God opened the door for me to speak to a number of other youths at a city prayer and worship gathering. As the event approached, I asked God how He wanted me to prepare for sharing such a message. First, I felt that God directed my heart toward a particular subject and a few specific Scriptures. But most importantly, He directed me toward taking a time of sabbath rest with Him so that I would be prepared for Him to minister through me.

The week before the event our school had a break from classes for one week. This was usually a great time to have fun, stay busy with friends, and engage in a lot of activities that required free time. However, the Lord had other plans. God wanted me to learn sabbath rest. For the whole week, I felt the Lord encouraging me to avoid social activity. He urged me not to schedule any activities, and He called me to put off time with friends until the next week. The week was a time to rest in the Lord and allow Him to prepare me and to fill me with what He knew I needed.

I will never forget that week of sabbath with the Lord. I learned to cease from my activity and allow Him to be active in my life!

He blessed me with more than I could imagine. He filled me up, and then, as I spoke at the event, He poured Himself out in a way that only He could. When we take a sabbath with the Lord, it is a time to decrease so that He can increase. God moved on my behalf that week and has done the same many other times since, when I give Him my time.

It is the same process when we try and join God in the streets with the steps of love from Isaiah 58. Each week God asks us to intentionally set aside a time to Sabbath with Him. When we take this time we are filled up, overflowing with the joy of the Lord, and ready to join Him where He is moving.

Sabbath rest has changed our lives, more than once.

APPLICATION

- Read and pray through the following Scriptures that have to do with sabbath rest: Psalms 46:10; Hebrews 4:10; Exodus 16:29; Zechariah 4:6; Isaiah 40:31; Isaiah 49:23.

- When can you intentionally set aside time this week as a day of sabbath rest and refilling with the Lord?

- What must you do to protect this time with the Lord?

- Where do you need to go to maximize this time?

- Think and pray ahead about what is necessary so that the busyness of life does not get in the way of the discipline of sabbath rest.

- Enjoy the day of rest in and with the Lord.

- Allow God to fill you up with His best!

BEFORE YOU GO

Wait on the Lord

Just as we need to take a Sabbath for one day each week, we also must reserve some sabbath time with the Lord each day. I am always amazed at how rejuvenated and refreshed in the Lord I am when I cease from my daily activities and set apart a time just to wait on Him. It changes everything! He changes me!

STEP 12

Then you will find your joy in the LORD (Isaiah 58:14).

EXPLANATION

What I love about this verse is the word *then*. *Then* is a very simple word, but in this case, its meaning is extremely powerful. If we walk with God through this fast that He has chosen, *then* we will find our joy in Him. If we will walk with the Lord through these steps, we will be fasting from self. We won't look to fulfill selfish desires, but we will live out the kind of love that God desires.

Our joy in going to the marketplace won't be about what we will get for ourselves, but about whom God desires to bless there. We won't go to a restaurant or café looking to be fulfilled by taste or fullness, but by finding the person God wants to feed. We won't take walks outside just to get to work or to exercise, but to find the person to whom God wants to lead us that day. We will find our joy in the Lord because we will be joining Him where He is moving; we will look to fulfill His steps rather than our own. We will find our joy in the Lord because we will be with Him, and because we know that anything is possible *with* God. We will find joy in the Lord because our actions will be completely focused on loving Him with all our attention, and loving our neighbors as He gives us the direction. Then we will find joy in the Lord.

PRAYER

Lord, I love You with all my heart! I want to love You more; I know this includes loving those around me even as I love myself. Please help me to fulfill this fast from self by turning my selfish love outward to serve those around me. What I want to receive, please help me to give. The purpose I dream for, help me to pray forward for someone else. I want to be more like You, Jesus. Please help me, Holy Spirit, help me to live Your Word. Please help me to find joy in You. In Jesus's name I pray. Amen.

TESTIMONY

I will never forget a trip my wife, our daughter, and I took to Rwanda several years back. We had only one child at the time, our first biological daughter, Mercy. She was four when we took the trip. We had a very powerful time during the trip and saw God draw many people, including many children, to Himself.

However, there are one or two memories from the trip that stand out more than others. One day in particular we went to a church that was on an elementary school campus. We had an amazing time of prayer, encouragement, and worship with those involved. The part I remember most was a simple act of love that our four-year-old daughter demonstrated, one that brought us all joy.

The gathering had ended, and we were in the truck starting to drive away. As had happened on a number of occasions throughout the trip, many of the children chased our vehicle. Mercy looked down at the kids and saw their needs. She then looked down at herself and her bag full of school supplies, coloring books, and crafts. Without even asking us, this four-year-old started emptying her backpack and handing out every item she could. The moment was brief, but it lasted until her bag was empty. Mercy took some of the worldly things she found the most joy in and multiplied that joy tenfold. She found joy in the Lord as a result.

Mercy's whole outlook on life and many of her desires changed after that trip. Ever since, she has seen past herself to others and their needs despite her young age, which would seem to excuse her from selflessness. Perhaps the most special part is not that she learned to reach beyond herself, but that she found amazing joy in doing so. Her name, Mercy, is reflective of the fast God has called us to in Isaiah 58. She has not only shown us the power of love, but has been a great example of how to find God's joy in extending that love.

APPLICATION

Take some time in prayer to talk to the Lord. Let Him speak to your heart about what has taken place in your life during the previous 11 steps.

- Has God given you a new joy in Him?
- Do you find joy in Him as you extend His love in new ways?

- Ask God to show you another new friend or prayer partner He may be calling to take these steps.

- Take some time to pray for this person before you approach him or her.

- Set up a time to talk and pray with this friend and potential prayer partner.

- Share with this individual the new testimonies God has given you. Tell the person about the journey God has you on. Share ways in which God has moved during this journey. Explain how the Lord and His love have changed your life. Describe the joy you have found in the Lord.

- Show this friend and potential prayer partner the steps you have been taking through the map in Isaiah 58.

- Read the passage aloud together. Pray the passage aloud together!

- Spend time praying and waiting on the Lord together so He can direct you.

- Go, join the Lord, and live out the love of Isaiah 58 again, together.

BEFORE YOU GO

Wait on the Lord

We have talked about it before, and I must repeat it again. Take time each day to wait on the Lord. Seek God's help. Ask the Holy Spirit to fill you up. Allow Jesus to impart His love. The more we wait on the Lord, the more we know how to join Him.

And when we wait on the Lord, He gives us the strength to join Him. If we want to walk like Jesus across the map of Isaiah 58, we first must sit with Jesus and wait for Him to prepare us. Take some time to be alone with God and meditate on His Word. Take time to practice your intimate relationship with God.

CONCLUSION

DURING OUR TIME HERE in Addis Ababa, Ethiopia, we have gradually learned the local language called Amharic. We are so very thankful to many of our friends who have graciously and patiently taught us the language. For us, it has been much easier to learn the Amharic words for everyday phrases, places, and items of use than it has been to learn the Amharic for many of our favorite Bible promises or encouragements that we love to offer.

The Amharic phrase, *Eyesus mekaru zigujuno alleh,* (written phonetically), is one we have been taught; we have spoken it, we have prayed it, and we continue to take time to believe it each and every day. This saying is taken from John 4:34-35, and it is trans- lated: "Jesus says the harvest is ready!"

As we discussed previously, it does not matter whether you live in a city or nation that battles poverty and immense need, or a wealthy city or suburban area. No matter where you are, the harvest is plentiful. It is all around you—and Jesus says that it is ready. In fact, Jesus has shown us that it is ready by living out the passage from Isaiah 58 every day of His life in the streets and marketplaces that were all around Him.

It all comes down to perspective. It is difficult to walk out the door and see God's potential harvest when our eyes are on that which appeases self. But if we leave the threshold of our homes with eyes lifted up, searching to find the Lord's movement in the common streets and public areas that surround us, we will see a whole new world. We will find new opportunities and infinite possibilities to join with God. He is waiting for us to enter into this fast that He has chosen. God is waiting for us to see our world and even our ministries differently. He is waiting for us to join Him where He is already moving!

Wherever you are, whoever you are, and regardless of what you do or do not have, an incredible opportunity is before you. Today, you have the opportunity to walk out of your door and into the harvest fields Jesus describes. Each of us has the opportunity to join the Lord in His steps and to demonstrate His unending love— right beside Him!—toward the people He loves so dearly.

Isaiah 58 shows us a map of the kind of love God moves in. It is a map of the steps Jesus took. It shows us how we can pray and how we can join Him right now in gathering the harvest. We are presented with a fast from self, a fast of love that teaches us how to love like Jesus, *with Jesus,* everywhere we go.

Are you willing to take these steps with us? The world will be forever changed. *"Eyesus mekaru zigujuno alleh!"*

Jesus says the harvest is ready!

ENDNOTES

CHAPTER 1: THE PRISON

1. Laurie Klein, "I Love You, Lord," House of Mercy Music (Maranatha! Music [Admin. by the Copyright Company], 1978, 1980).

CHAPTER 2: THE WARDEN

1. See John 14:6.

CHAPTER 3: GIVING LIFE

1. 2 Cor. 12:9.
2. See Matthew 7:1-2.
3. See John 1:14.
4. See Hebrews 4:16.
5. See Genesis 3:6-12.
6. See John 15:19; 17:14-16.
7. See Second Timothy 4:8.

8. See Second Corinthians 12:9-10.

9. Jer. 15:19 (NASB).

10. See Genesis 1:26.

11. See Genesis 25 and 27.

12. See Genesis 27:34.

13. See John 8:32.

CHAPTER 5: THE INTERCESSOR

1. See Malachi 4:6.

2. See Romans 8:26.

3. See John 3:17.

4. See First John 4:18.

5. See Second Corinthians 5:7.

6. See Luke 6:28.

CHAPTER 8: HIDDEN TREASURES

1. See James 4:8.

2. See Galatians 5:22-23.

3. See John 15:16.

4. See John 15:5.

5. See Matthew 6:20.

CHAPTER 9: THE RED SEA

1. Matt. 7:7 NKJV.

2   See Isaiah 55:8-9.

3. See Galatians 2:20.

4. Heb. 13:5 NKJV.

5. See Second Corinthians 5:7.

6. See First Corinthians 10:13.

7. See Romans 8:28.

8. See Matthew 19:26.

9. See First John 4:18.

10. James 4:6.

CHAPTER 10: A TALL TOWER

1. See Genesis 50:20.

2. See John 14:12.

3. See Genesis 16.

4. See Genesis 15:4.

5. See Isaiah 55:8-9.

6. Heb. 6:12 NKJV.

7. See First Corinthians 2:9.

8. See Romans 8:28.

9. See Genesis 50:20.

CHAPTER 11: FREEDOM?

1. See Second Corinthians 5:7.

2. See Isaiah 58:6.

3. Isa. 58:9 NKJV.

4. Isa. 58:6 NKJV.

5. Isa. 58:7 NKJV.

6. Isa. 58:10 NKJV.

7. Isaiah 58:6 NKJV.

8. See Isaiah 58:7.

9. Isa. 58:9 NKJV.

10. Isa. 58:12 NKJV.

11. Isa. 58:10 NKJV.

12. Ps. 34:8.

13. 2 Cor. 3:17.

14. Isa. 58:9 NKJV.

15. A variation of Matthew 6:24.

16. See Isaiah 55:8-9.

17. See Isaiah 43:18-19.

18. See Matthew 7:13-14.

19. See First John 4:4.

APPENDIX

1. *Dictionary.com Unabridged, Random House, Inc.,* Dictionary. com, s.v. "oppress," http://dictionary.reference.com/browse/oppress (accessed: February 20, 2011).

2. See Proverbs 3:5-6.

ABOUT JOEY LETOURNEAU

Joey LeTourneau is 29 years old and lives in Addis Ababa, Ethiopia with his wife, Destiny, and their four daughters: Anna, Aynalem, Mercy, and Galilee. He works with Heavenly Hope Ministries to coordinate M.A.R.K. 10:14, a movement focused on gathering into the Father's arms the poor, broken, and empty children of Ethiopia, other African nations, and beyond. They are believing God for each child to be released from bondage, transformed by love, and empowered by the Spirit to be sons and daughters of the Most High God. Joey has grown up in full-time ministry, picking up this mantle when he was 18 years old. He has traveled extensively, speaking in the U.S. and internationally, empowering the Body of Christ to draw near to their First Love, hear His voice, and join God in the purposes He has created them for.

E-mail: joey.letourneau@gmail.com
Facebook: Revolutionary Freedom
Web: www.mark1014family.com

In the right hands, This Book will Change Lives!

Most of the people who need this message will not be looking for this book. To change their lives, you need to put a copy of this book in their hands.

> *But others (seeds) fell into good ground, and brought forth fruit, some a hundred-fold, some sixty-fold, some thirty-fold* (Matthew 13:8).

Our ministry is constantly seeking methods to find the good ground, the people who need this anointed message to change their lives. Will you help us reach these people?

> *Remember this—a farmer who plants only a few seeds will get a small crop. But the one who plants generously will get a generous crop* (2 Corinthians 9:6).

EXTEND THIS MINISTRY BY SOWING
3 BOOKS, 5 BOOKS, 10 BOOKS, OR MORE TODAY,
AND BECOME A LIFE CHANGER!

Thank you,

Don Nori Sr., Founder
Destiny Image
Since 1982

DESTINY IMAGE PUBLISHERS, INC.

*"Speaking to the Purposes of God for This Generation
and for the Generations to Come."*

VISIT OUR NEW SITE HOME AT
WWW.DESTINYIMAGE.COM

FREE SUBSCRIPTION TO DI NEWSLETTER

Receive free unpublished articles by top DI authors, exclusive

discounts, and free downloads from our best and newest books.

Visit www.destinyimage.com to subscribe.

Write to: Destiny Image
              P.O. Box 310
              Shippensburg, PA 17257-0310

Call: 1-800-722-6774

Email: orders@destinyimage.com

For a complete list of our titles or to place an order
online, visit www.destinyimage.com.